I FELT THE END BEFORE IT CAME

ALSO BY DANIEL ALLEN COX

Mouthquake

Basement of Wolves

Krakow Melt

Shuck

I FELT THE END BEFORE IT CAME

Memoirs
of a Queer
Ex-Jehovah's
Witness

DANIEL ALLEN COX

VIKING

VIKING

an imprint of Penguin Canada, a division of Penguin Random House Canada Limited

Canada • USA • UK • Ireland • Australia • New Zealand • India • South Africa • China

First published 2023

www.penguinrandomhouse.ca

LIBRARY AND ARCHIVES CANADA CATALOGUING IN PUBLICATION

Title: I felt the end before it came : memoirs of a queer ex-Jehovah's Witness / Daniel Allen Cox.
Names: Cox, Daniel Allen, author.
Identifiers: Canadiana (print) 20220233020 | Canadiana (ebook) 20220233055 |
ISBN 9780735242104 (hardcover) | ISBN 9780735242111 (EPUB)
Subjects: LCSH: Cox, Daniel Allen. | LCSH: Cox, Daniel Allen—Childhood and youth. | LCSH: Ex-church members—Jehovah's Witnesses. | LCSH: Ex-church members—Canada—Biography. | LCSH: Gay men—Canada—Biography. | CSH: Authors, Canadian (English)—21st century—Biography. | LCGFT: Autobiographies. | LCGFT: Creative nonfiction.
Classification: LCC BX8526.5 .C69 2023 | DDC 289.9/2092—dc23

Cover and interior design by Matthew Flute
Cover photograph by Stanley Stellar

Printed in Canada

10 9 8 7 6 5 4 3 2 1

 Penguin
Random House
VIKING CANADA

For Ian Huggins and Stephen Nelson,
and for Kevin Killian

If he had a computer, Jesse thought, and wasn't a
Jehovah's Witness, he would write a book about his
childhood. Jehovah's Witnesses don't write books.

—PAUL MENDEZ, *RAINBOW MILK*

CONTENTS

THE LETTER

Most know Jehovah's Witnesses as the people who stand on street corners with literature carts, telling strangers they can live forever on a *Paradise earth*. They're the neighbours who believe that at Armageddon—which is coming any day now—Jehovah and his son, Jesus, will literally kill billions of non-Witnesses and leave their bodies to rot in the street. They don't vote because the *new world* that follows will make elections obsolete. Others know them as the patients in hospitals who refuse blood transfusions at the risk of death. They're the ever-smiling Christians who don't celebrate birthdays and who don't send their kids to university because they would be better served by studying *The Watchtower*, the flagship magazine of the Watch Tower Society, the group that controls all Witness life and is the sole source for what it calls *the truth*.

I, on the other hand, will always know the Witnesses— JWs for short—as the people who watched as I was baptized at age thirteen in an inflatable Canadian Tire pool in a minor league hockey arena at the group's 1989 district convention in Ottawa. I shivered in the waist-deep water, marvelled at the utter cheapness of the pool, and thought, *This must be the way to Paradise.* Two hunks in clingy swimwear and white T-shirts grabbed and dunked me. Later, when friends and family asked if I'd felt anything, I said I did, but it wasn't the feeling they thought it was.

That year, I carried a Bible through the halls of St. Pius X High School, tucked under my arm with my textbooks. Catholics often mistook me for one of them, and on my shyer and weaker days, I let this misconception go. I sometimes brought an *Awake!* magazine to science class, the last place you'd expect to find a creationist periodical. It might've been a ploy my mother and I concocted to inure me to lies; the mere presence of Witness literature would act as an antidote to *false teachings* like evolution. But mostly I carried the literature to *give a good witness.*

I preached door to door after school and on weekends, sometimes with other Witnesses but often alone. This *good news of the Kingdom* we dropped in the snow, shoved into hands, and jimmied into doors to prevent them from closing. We targeted the weak, the sick, the old, the war-weary, the grieving, and anyone else looking for comfort and stability. We called on mansions to tell the people who lived there that the Paradise they thought they'd already found wasn't going to last. Our job was to rescue people from dying at Armageddon. We did this work for free because it was our privilege to do so. We charged householders a small fee for the books and magazines, until we were told to ask for donations instead. We dropped this money into the contribution box, along with money of our own. Jehovah was watching, so we always made sure to slip in a few bills among the coins. Our salvation depended on it.

In election years, I used openers like "We're asking your neighbours if they think politicians tell the truth" and "Can mankind's governments really offer lasting solutions to our problems?" My audience often slammed the door, but I still racked up an impressive number of return visits. I checked the boxes on the field service sheets: Not at Home, Call Again, or Do Not Call. The last was reserved for hostile encounters, in which householders told us to leave and never come back. Sometimes they proclaimed we were in a cult, a comment we were trained to expect. That's exactly what someone would say if they were controlled by Satan and angry that we had the one true religion.

The truth is a boot camp where kids and converts are taught a unique lexicon. Jehovah's Witnesses don't speak in tongues, but their sociolect is dense enough that you can have difficulty understanding them when they thrust literature at you and tell you it's *food at the proper time.* The Watch Tower knows exactly when to spoon-feed doctrine to its followers, and this sociolect is a kind of food they learn to crave. There was no room to interpret the Scriptures on our own. Doing so meant we were *relying on our own understanding,* and we could be disciplined for that. Understanding could come only from Jehovah in the form of *new light.* As long as I remained a good Christian, my path would be lit. At least the next few feet of it, anyway.

———

We didn't have a word to describe a parental body falling through space. The event renders language unusable to the child, the bystander, the witness. At age ten I watched as my mother staggered and told me she couldn't see, then fell on the bed and asked me to call 911. I dialed, but didn't know what to say, so I pressed the phone into her hand. I would later find out she was going into shock. I could hear in the subtext of what she explained to the operator that it was more than just a physical problem. With us, there was always a spiritual component.

She hemorrhaged most of her blood that day. It was her spiritual duty as a Jehovah's Witness to refuse transfusions, because of the sacredness of blood. At this very moment, somewhere in the world, a set of JW parents are seated in court, flipping through Leviticus, explaining why their sick kid can't have blood while the judge wonders how long they can afford to debate religious freedom. A small life ebbs away under a web of tubing.

Hospital staff did what they could to keep my mother's veins from collapsing. I spent three weeks gazing at her through the polyethylene screen of her ICU tent. She was anemic and turning yellow, buried under the equipment, eyes half open. The JW Hospital Liaison Committee arrived with briefcases full of legal precedent and defended my mother's right to bloodless treatment. I don't remember whether she received plasma substitutes or nothing at all. Ultimately, the committee defended her right to die.

My uncle and I discovered a broken vending machine that returned all the money when you bought a drink. Most visitors to the hospital didn't realize it, and we fleeced them while they drowned their grief in pop. My family assumed—wrongly—that I was terrified. I was oblivious, either weighing dimes by the pound or reading the fine print on the "No Blood" card I had to carry with me. If I ever ended up in the same position as my mom, I would have to assert my faith and reject any transfusion the doctors pushed on me. If my little body couldn't handle it and I came to an earthly end, then so be it. I would be resurrected in Paradise. It was a win-win. In the waiting room, I did my homework to the white noise of machine bleeps. I still feel guilty for not being afraid. Was I showing faith or ignorance? Neither is quite right.

Late nights at home with my stepdad were too quiet. He just stared at me, probably in disbelief that he might have to raise a kid by himself. What did kids eat, think, dream, and obsess over? Did we mind secondhand smoke? One night, it hit him hard. "Do you realize how close she is to dying?" he asked me. "Do you have any idea at all?" His questions were supposed to slap me aware. The moment was all about him.

My stepdad sometimes came to meetings, but he just as often skipped them. I don't know what he thought about my mother's decision to abstain from blood. I just didn't want to be left alone with him. I'd feared his angry outbursts for years. He and my mom fought constantly, and he levelled his rage against both of us. At least with my mom there to protect me,

I'd be okay. What a selfish thing for me to think, as if my mom's everlasting salvation weren't more important.

My mom was transferred to a semi-private room where she was allowed to eat non-hospital food. My aunts arrived with an industrial juicer and made her beet and carrot sludge for the iron content. They ground incessantly. I can still smell the mulch they left in the juicer between rounds. My mother, the Bloodless Miracle, gradually got better. The nurses crossed themselves when she walked out.

Why hadn't I worried about losing my mother? I'm hoping the answer isn't because I believed—that isn't the narrative I've constructed for myself since the days of beet juice and prayer. For my mother, surviving this brush with death is a point of pride, vindication for having remained faithful to Witness law. This is the type of thing that embeds religion within families and makes it shameful to abandon.

———

In 1982 my mother took me to see the film *Deathtrap*, a dark comedy starring Christopher Reeve and Michael Caine, in which they infamously share a kiss. I know my mother covered my eyes at certain points, but not during the kiss, because I remember seeing it. It got a rise out of the people around us in the theatre. If she'd known the kiss was coming, we wouldn't have gone to see *Deathtrap*. It would be years before I would ascribe anything sexual to Reeve, when I would stare at the bulge in Superman's red undies on the faded movie posters and know what to do with the feeling. I suspect my mother has since revisited the scenario of our day at the theatre and hypothesized on the effect the kiss had on me. I wonder if she blames herself, even though the blame is a credit, and one she cannot possibly earn. My queerness is worth more than the cost of a movie ticket in 1982.

For JWs, queerness is a sin that leads to destruction at Armageddon. "Homosexuality is not an alternative life-style acceptable to Jehovah God," says *The Watchtower*. "Frequently, both gay and liberal preachers twist the scriptures in futile endeavors to make it seem that it is." It was the sin of Sodom and Gomorrah, committed by those whom the apostle Paul called "unreasoning animals born naturally to be caught and destroyed." I had every reason to believe that at the appointed time Jehovah and Jesus would smite me to pieces and leave my bones for the birds. If, outwardly, my baptism marked my dedication to Jehovah, inwardly it marked a sexual bubbling. *Questions Young People Ask—Answers That Work*, released the same weekend I was baptized, says that avoiding hugging your "same-sex friends" quashes any "homosexual feelings" you may have toward them. I tested the theory out: false.

I hid my queerness for years. I knew there was something wrong with me because the books and magazines told me so. Jehovah was a straight alpha male, a model for every man and boy in His organization. I was eventually supposed to find a wife to knock on doors with until we'd rapped the skin off our knuckles. We would spawn entire congregations of children: boys who would marry girls, and girls who would marry boys. But the elders somehow knew I was different. I could feel the accusations in their talks from the podium, the way their eyes would land on me as they spoke of aberrations, of unclean and unnatural desires. And they had a point. Because afterward, when I stripped off my meeting suit and took to the shower, I would think about men and the totally unnatural ways I could touch them. And just when the feeling peaked, I would hear the voices of condemnation and try to hold back, and in the trying I would cum harder each time. I spent half my teenage years sitting in shame in a cold bathtub, wondering why my dick was hard but my religious zeal was going soft.

By the time I was eighteen I'd started sneaking out of my parents' apartment in the West Island suburbs of Montreal to make the two-hour trip downtown by bus and metro.

I sought refuge at Sky, the biggest club in the gay village, where I shook my ass to house music and let older men chase me from one dance floor to another. One night I got drunk on sugary cocktails and saw him dancing: a boy made of moves and mischief. I found holes in the matrix of elbows and slipped closer to him. Drew from Connecticut, he said. The music changed and I went for it—our kiss was a detonation and it cleared a ten-minute space around us. He took me back to the hotel where he was staying with friends, who minded their own business while we made out in the bath for six hours, and by minded their own business I mean listened at the door. Drew knew he was my first and took his time kissing me while the bathwater turned cold. I was lost in the world of his eyes, his tongue, the stubble that scratched my face raw. We didn't sleep and nor did we fuck; the Paradise of his mouth was enough for me.

Every time I returned to the village, I was struck by the AIDS ribbons on trees, sun-faded and wind-torn, and by the body outlines painted on Rue Sainte-Catherine to mark murders of people like me. Being gay could kill me before Armageddon came—unless this was the proof that it was already here. Regardless, I soon started having more sex, often with older men. Some seemed hesitant to touch me, aware of the delicate crossroads I'd reached. Others fucked me with abandon. I loved it all. For many of these men, it was the first time they had ever let a Jehovah's Witness inside the house. The Watch Tower literature was clear: "No apologies, no concessions, no ambiguity— homosexuality is detestable in God's sight." *But what if God can't see?* I thought. Slipping into bed with men felt so right. Each time, I stumbled a little further away from Jehovah. I started building a theology of queer tenderness. Nerve endings don't split on ridges of good and evil. Pleasure cascades down both sides. I think part of me dismissed the risk of getting caught, because no pious Christian in any position to report me would be hanging out openly in Montreal's gay village, would they? Another part of me realized it was inevitable that my secret would get out. Maybe I wanted to be caught.

One evening I was bowling with my friend Natalya, her boyfriend, and a few others from my congregation, throw- ing strikes until the end of the world. I casually told Natalya that her boyfriend was handsome, and she just nodded. A day later, my home phone rang. It was my congregation's presiding elder, asking if I was "a homosexual." I knew that Orwellian surveillance was a fine-tuned fruit machine and figured out that someone had told on me (either Natalya or someone she'd told), but the call still came as a surprise.

Normally, Witnesses are made to account for any wrong-doing in person before a judicial committee of elders. The fact that my hearing occurred over the phone was an anomaly, and I still can't explain it. When he said the word *homosexual*, it was the first time anyone had named me that way, and it felt true. The feeling had been building for some time, to the degree that it no longer seemed I had a place at the Kingdom Hall. My meeting attendance had dropped, and I'd stopped going out in field service altogether. The awareness within me had begun to boil, to stretch the seams of the person I was supposed to be. I was ready to say yes; I assured the elder of my proclivity for and deepening knowledge of all things homo, but before I could delve into the glories of queer sex he cut me off and gave me two formal options: *disfellowshipping* or *disassociation*. Either way, I would be forced to choose between sucking dick or swallowing the firehose of the word of God.

Disfellowshipping is a form of JW discipline reserved for serious transgressions of the rules, often of a sexual nature—premarital, oral, or anal sex, even between husband and wife; adultery; "homosexual activity"; and the catch-all, "loose conduct"—basically anything that deviates from hetero-married-missionary. Disfellowshipping is also the customary punishment for anybody caught smoking, *fornicating*, ingesting blood, celebrating *worldly* holidays, practising spiritism, and many other offences. JW disciplinary rules often shift, so this list is subject to change.

When a Witness is disfellowshipped—sometimes whether they are repentant or not—they can't speak to any other congregation members, including family, save for exceptional circumstances. They lose many of their friends, suffer silently at the dinner table, and are ordered to slink out of meetings before the closing song to avoid interacting with anybody. The JWs believe this policy is kindness, not cruelty, that shunning will teach the disfellowshipped person a lesson and encourage them to repent. Curiously, Witnesses refuse to admit that they "shun," and instead prefer euphemisms like "we don't associate with this person," as if there were a difference.

Vulnerable people are separated from their communities at the exact time they need them. If the disfellowshipped person manages to endure a year of this without a total mental health breakdown or dying by suicide, and if they still think that a group that doesn't acknowledge their existence is worth the wait, then they can be *reinstated*. Endure an emotionally wrecking year of abuse, and you get to come back. Shunning is central to the Watch Tower Society, one of the tools it uses to obtain obedience and consolidate power.

Disassociation sounded like a better option to me. Unlike disfellowshipping, it's a voluntary exit. When a JW disassociates, there are no conditions. There is no grovelling. The sinner proclaims themselves an unredeemable spirit, an *apostate*, a force that is poisonous to other Witnesses, and they don't come back. Shunning an apostate is a way for active members to confirm their choice to remain. It allows the community the option of punishing a single member rather than becoming self-aware.

The elder who phoned me must have seen other young Jehomos ripen under his watch, because he seemed to know I was a lost cause. He ended the call by saying, "I love you, be careful of AIDS." If this was love, it was weaponized. So, not love at all. I wrote a letter in pen and on looseleaf and mailed it either to the elder's house or to the Kingdom Hall, I don't remember which. I forget the words and didn't make any copies, but I know it's the best thing I've ever written, a planet forming in a cloud of dust, the language of goodbye infused with desire. It was a breakup letter to Jehovah, the first proof I've ever had that I could think for myself.

I don't know where I got the strength to write this letter. It couldn't be Christian fortitude because that was the very thing I was rebelling against. My strength couldn't have come from self-knowledge because I remained a mystery to myself. I had no queer role models to tell me things would be all right on the outside. The letter could only have been a feeling: a desperation, a soul leak, a horniness for a future that made sense. It was a scroll I would understand only much later, even though it was lost the minute I dropped it in the mailbox.

Sending the letter set off a chain reaction—I had to speak to my mother before that Tuesday's meeting, before they announced my departure and she found out publicly that her son was going to die at Armageddon. Better to hear the news from me. Because of our schedules, I had to come out to her from a pay phone while I was waiting for the bus. So this was what the end times felt like: fishing for a quarter in the 'burbs, hands shaking. When she picked up, I told her I was leaving *the truth*. The entire future of our relationship played out in the few seconds I waited for her reaction. She cried, and I could tell she already knew. I broke her heart, this woman who had risked her life for the religion she saw fit to raise me in.

This happened over twenty-five years ago, but the pain is still fresh. There are so many things I couldn't have known at the time, such as how the letter was only the first of many I would write, and that I would forever be leaving the Jehovah's Witnesses; how I would embark on a lifetime project to redefine words that had once been used against me. We will always be living between languages, between one describing a familiar world and one describing the inchoate self, too new to be understood. The point is that one cannot imagine escape, or agency, or the true shape of one's life until there is a language for it.

The more words I redefined, the less certain I was about anything, including the difference between *in* and *out*. And none of my departures were as simple as they had first seemed.

THE GLOW OF ELECTRUM

There's no guarantee that a stutterer can say their own name. I routinely slip down the rounded edge of my own first initial, unable to climb it easily. When I was younger and someone asked for my name, I sometimes gave them an alias, thinking myself clever to be Eric or Ian or Oliver— free of the consonant I was born with—until I got stuck in the glue trap of the vowel I'd chosen. Now, getting my name out can take a second. A lifetime in speech years. Everyone reads the delay differently. *Don't say Stuttering, say Childhood Onset Fluency Disorder.* (Thank you, American Psychiatric Association. I'll use whichever comes out first.)

My mouth became a locus of shame at the Kingdom Hall. To "pass into the kingdom of heaven" is not to "pass through the eye of a needle," as the Bible says, but rather through the obstacle course of my mouth. My face contorted when I blocked and my sibilants hissed to a messy end. When I tried to avoid answering questions during Bible study, various congregation members would remind me that Moses had an "infirmity of speech" and that I should be brave and patient. I was told that in Paradise, my stutter would be cured. I was supposed to be grateful that Jehovah loved me *despite* my speech.

In order to *give a good witness* when we preached door to door, we were supposed to be eloquent, mellifluous. After all, we were ambassadors of Jehovah, and it would reflect badly on Him if we hesitated when speaking to householders, as if we weren't sure of the message we brought them. The *Theocratic Ministry School Guidebook*, which we studied to refine our preaching skills, told us that "the more common causes of lack of fluency are lack of clear thinking and preparation of the material. It can also result from a weak vocabulary or a poor choice of words . . . There, the problem is particularly serious, because in some instances, your audience will literally walk out on you."

I gave my first Bible talk when I was thirteen, just before I was baptized. I read from the Book of Ezekiel and explained what it meant, eager to show what I'd learned by reading *The Watchtower* magazine. I stood at a wooden lectern that was stained by the sweaty hands of first talks. My own wet fingers stuck to the onionskin Bible pages as I turned to Ezekiel Chapter 38. I would have preferred to read from a vision in Chapter 1. "And their appearance and their structure were just as when a wheel proved to be in the midst of a wheel . . . And I got to see something like the glow of electrum." This is exactly what you'd find if you looked inside my mouth: wheels inside wheels and electrum, an unholy alloy of silver, gold, and traces of copper. You would see the mechanisms of the *betweenness* of stuttering. It is where words fail that language truly begins.

As I expounded from the podium, an elder graded my performance by checking off boxes on the Speech Counsel Sheet.

Volume. (Was I expounding loudly enough?)
Pausing. (Perhaps once too often?)
Repetition for Emphasis. (You've got to be kidding me.)
Fluency. (A word I no longer use. Well, not really.)
Timing. (You have no idea what I'm building to, in the
shadow of that mountain of a word.)

The Speech Counsel Sheet was the ultimate scrutiny. There was no more hellish panopticon for a stutterer. And it showed ignorance because the points it listed had no nuance. Not all hesitations are composed of the same materials. Some are opaque, others a barely perceptible half-step. A filler word can sound like the real thing. Sometimes the body continues moving through a word; the mouth freezes but the foot taps on. Or the body can get stuck as the bridge between two concepts, a stop-motion work of art. Whatever the case, to observe a stutterer is to time travel.

The Tetragrammaton, transliterated as YHWH or JHVH in the Roman alphabet, appears in the Bible over seven thousand times. Those who say it's unpronounceable aren't used to substituting more difficult sounds for easier ones. A stutterer is always ready with a letter replacement. We can make shit up in the first few seconds of trouble.

Silences, however, can be squeaks, evasions, hums, or teeth chatters, and not silences at all. They are always embarrassing. When a stutterer tries to insert a meaningful pause—an intentional hesitation—it reads as just another stutter, and often, as indecision. I feel that Leonard Cohen understood this when he wrote that his silences were accused of being just another form of poetry.

I somehow got through my Bible reading. My white dress shirt was soaked with sweat. I watched the elder mark "Work on This," "Improved," or "Good" beside the boxes on the sheet as he decided whether I had a voice befitting a messenger of God. I'm certain I stuttered, but I don't remember where. Maybe my entire discourse was a blockage. Maybe the audience attributed any smoothness on my part to assistance from Jehovah, as if the words of the prophet Ezekiel transformed my larynx, mouth, and tongue and healed me on their way out. "You are not being sent to many peoples speaking an unintelligible language or an unknown tongue, whose words you cannot understand. If I would send you to them, they would listen to you." Why couldn't I have been raised in a church that spoke in tongues? Then my glossolalia would at least be worth something.

———

The promise of Paradise didn't stop my mother from taking me to speech therapy when I was around twelve. After all, there was still preaching to do, and I was a defective missionary. Kids made fun of me at school and mimicked my anguished "stutter face"—what I perceived as my ugliness reflected. Maybe therapy and the fluency it seemed to promise could help me blend in socially a little better.

Paula, a speech therapist at the Montreal Children's Hospital, sat at a low table and smiled widely to make herself as kidlike and unthreatening as possible. Her office walls were covered in colourful posters that showed the body parts involved in producing speech. In our sessions, she demystified the collaboration between diaphragm and lungs, jaw and nasal passage. As part of my exercises I had to lightly touch my tongue to the fillings in my top and bottom teeth, some of them silver, and perhaps electrum itself.

Paula's fluency-shaping program operated on a theory that middle ear muscles interfere with the timing of "auditory feedback"—how the speaker hears their own voice. So she made me speak into a flexible straw stuck in my ear, as if I were an igneous intrusion—a former volcano with interrupted lava flow—and she wanted me to listen to the rumblings. What I heard were spit bubbles. The therapy also included "gentle onset": you approach a consonant with a slow buildup of voice. This helps avoid a block. "Do it breathy, like Marilyn Monroe," Paula told me. She assigned me homework. I asked random questions of shopkeepers and other strangers, and heavy-breathed my way through telephone fact-finding missions. Marilyn, it turns out, was also a stutterer.

I fell away from speech therapy ever so gradually, as gently as Paula had taught me to approach words—or tried to. The therapy hadn't delivered the promised results. Maybe

I had simply outgrown the Children's Hospital. I'm sure the service was valuable to many kids my age, stutterers and non-stutterers alike, and I didn't want to take that away from them. But walking out of the hospital for the last time, I felt the beginnings of a new thought: *What if there were nothing wrong with my speech?* What if, once I allowed strangeness of speech back into my life, my inner, unchecked narrative could finally flourish? What if, unmoored from expectation and without the strain of overcorrection, ideas could come out in the shape they needed to? At the time, I wasn't mature enough to phrase things this way, although these realizations still resounded through me. I used my straw to listen to the natural rhythms of my breath. It was a Cohen-like opening. There was indeed a crack in everything, starting with my speech.

I would eventually forget Paula's voice completely. That had been her goal: to make sure I could hear only my own. She was a *worldly* person, someone outside our JW bubble. Did that mean she wanted me to forget Jehovah's voice, too?

———

I noticed something curious at the weekly meetings when we belted out hymns from *Sing Praises to Jehovah*, the piano thundering through our middle ears: I didn't stutter when I sang. Neither had Marilyn.

Around the age of sixteen, I started an alternative rock band with two of my congregation friends, Myles and Danny. We hung out after meetings, usually in the basement of Danny's parents' house, and soon picked up on one another's musical sensibilities. Making music was allowed in the Jehovah's Witnesses, if we didn't try to emulate non-JW singers. (It was easy for us to keep the sex and drugs out of our rock and roll because we had neither.) Now my preferred magazines were *Billboard* and *Pitchfork* and its Canadian equivalent, *Chart*.

We called ourselves The Sixth Sense. Danny played bass, and Myles and I both played guitar. We bought a set of second-hand drums and took turns whacking them, not realizing the skins were busted. We paid out of pocket for hours at the recording studio—the same one where Céline Dion rehearsed in secret—and we obsessed over effects and fader levels, trying to create the kind of mystical experience we'd been taught could only be found through the Holy Spirit. We turned to music for transcendence instead of to Jehovah. We wrote our sad-boy indie songs in the bus terminal at Fairview Mall and became famous in the confines of a single West Island garage, elevated by singers whose brilliance we could never match.

When Pink Floyd announced they were coming to Olympic Stadium, Danny and I camped in the parking lot of Fairview Mall overnight to wait for tickets, smoking weed and drinking Southern Comfort in the bitter cold of February while security followed us from tent to tent. This contravened the rules of not only Fairview, but also the JWs. I was eighteen and already used to taking these kinds of risks, and I knew how to mask the smells of smoke and booze with air freshener and cheap colognes.

At the concert a few months later, we grew ever more comfortably numb under the giant inflatable pigs that floated overhead. With their album *The Wall*, Pink Floyd had dreamt of separation between band and world. I dreamt of separation between my musical life and my spiritual one, a separation that seemed somewhat far off. As I looked around the stadium, that leftover of the 1960s obsession with architectural geometry, now a crumbling death trap, I saw the 1978 Jehovah's Witness district convention where I fell off a yellow folding seat and took a nosedive into the concrete, opening a gash over my left eye. It remains my deepest scar. I looked a little further afield and saw myself at the 1988 convention, which copied the Olympic opening ceremonies by parading delegations from around the world. I'd waved to a group from Greece and cried because I knew

I was supposed to feel the swell of emotion, not because I truly felt it. Is there a difference?

But all of that evaporated by the time Pink Floyd played their encore and filled our heads with stars. When it was over, I refused a ride from Myles and chose to walk— alone—the five hours home along the river on the north shore. I arrived in the West Island at dawn a slightly different person.

The Sixth Sense was hostage to its influences. We wanted to be original, but sounding too much like the bands we listened to was a constant menace. I was just happy to have created a world where staccato attacks came from the instruments I played, not from my mouth. And at least we weren't Christian rock. At some point, every band asks themselves: Is our "sound" the sound we're actually making? Judging by the criteria on the Speech Counsel Sheet, I was sure we'd nailed it.

Enthusiasm. (We mistook the hormones of
puberty for genius.)
Warmth, Feeling. (Southern Comfort in a tent, anyone?)
Confidence and Poise. (We named our debut cassette
You Are Now Halfway to the Equator, unaware that
we were halfway to nowhere.)

Now, when I listen to our music on the single, warbly cassette that remains of our recording sessions, I can hear moments of yearning for escape amid a whole lot of mediocrity. The songs are rife with cliché 90s rock imagery, bad rhymes, and descriptions of utopia I'm afraid are more closely aligned to Witness teachings than to the freedom I was reaching for. But there's a line that haunts and encourages me:

Sometimes the only way to know is to feel.

I now recognize that I was trying to create a mythology, through lyrics and arrangements, that was as complex and encompassing as the one the Witnesses had created and then policed. In other words, our wild bouts of flange and distortion, our meandering solos, our naked cynicism—it was all impenetrable to the Watch Tower. Music created the new neural pathways I needed to finally think for myself. I could use it to orchestrate myself out of the Society's cultlike grip, one note at a time. And what had led me to music was my stutter, which was important to the Witnesses because it was how they could control and manipulate me. They wanted to stamp out any queer sounds.

What all this tells me is that music and stuttering are as key to the story of my departure from the Jehovah's Witnesses as queerness and sex are, even though each of these elements has the capacity to feel singular and definitive in terms of generating freedom for me. I might have to learn to be okay with not knowing the full reason I'm doing something—or how it's connected to the other somethings—until long after I do it.

———

My jaw hurts as I type this, as if I'm reliving four decades of stutters. My face retains the pressure of every contortion. I've put my night guard on in the middle of the day to prevent my teeth from grinding. I keep taking it out to sip coffee. Did my stutter grow in proportion to my mouth? It's difficult to know because nobody will tell me. I have bad days when I don't stutter at all and I feel like an impostor.

I cannot rid myself of the urge to play again. An inherited acoustic guitar sits atop one of my bookshelves, a taunt. I often find myself gazing up at it—the dusty curves, the wood panels where someone's palm sweat has soaked through. Sometimes before a writing session, I'll blast music and sing out the scenes until I'm hoarse and my soul shakes with joy. If some degree of Witness-think is a chronic condition in me—and I believe that to be the case—maybe I need music in my life forever as a buffer between me and the thinking I can't expel.

In "The (Loud) Soundtrack to My Struggle with Faith," Anna Gazmarian writes about grappling with her evangelical upbringing and finding solace in screamo music— in how "the incoherent lyrics and reckless drum solos reminded me of the gnashing of teeth, which the New Testament deploys as a statement of grief. This was the closest I came to worshipping God in years." I wonder about the nature of my own sixth sense, if I can ever hear music without feeling religious, if I can ever seek light that doesn't come from above.

The hard "j" is an affricate phoneme; to say "Jehovah" is to start with a blockage, followed by a coronal consonant, the flexible tip of the tongue releasing into audible friction. I've always had a hard time getting it out, as if stuttering has blessed me with the inability to say the name that has caused me the most pain. I think I'm finally ready to admit that the Tetragrammaton is unpronounceable.

Cohen gave us an alternative and put it into our mouths. We atheists can sing it the loudest. *Hallelujah.* The night he died, my partner Mark and I walked to his apartment without knowing why. Hundreds of other Montrealers had the same idea. We laid incense and rusty guitars and chrysanthemums and albums and books and bottles of whisky and a fedora on his steps because the music made us do it. Music is endemic to certain islands; Montreal is an island, and so are we. The kids drank wine at the corner of Rue Marie-Anne until morning. We sang songs, not realizing they were Buddhist chants, and waited for the cold peal of dawn.

When I got home, I picked up the guitar on my bookshelf, a stutter in my throat.

KINGDOM OF MEN

The Jehovah's Witnesses are run by a conglomerate of men: the Governing Body, district overseers, circuit overseers, ministerial servants, and congregation elders, each more stubborn than the next. None can ever admit to being wrong about prophecy, doctrine, or matters of organizational business, because to do so would be to admit that their relationship to God is no more privileged than anyone else's. At one of the JW conventions I attended as a kid, I basked in the heavenly voice of Brother Franz, president of the Watch Tower Society and as close to Jehovah as we could get, while he, nearly blind, trilled pronouncements that echoed terribly, not because the stadium acoustics were bad but because we had yet to develop the spiritual wisdom to properly receive Franz's message. My grandfather Keith apparently knew him. "His voice has the ring of truth," Grandpa would say.

I came even closer to greatness when Brother Twan, a circuit overseer, visited our apartment for lunch with his wife, and a few years later, when the even more revered Brother Nichol sat down for a bowl of my mother's famous lentil soup with his own wife in tow. He praised the soup and between spoonfuls doled out spiritual wisdom, which we lapped up. Brother Nichol would eventually give the talk that preceded my baptism. As I listened to him speak about the future that the pool a few metres away guaranteed, I wondered if the lentil soup would forever connect Brother Nichol and me in a spiritual way.

It wasn't an accident that Sister Twan and Sister Nichol were mostly quiet when they came to lunch. According to Jehovah's Witness doctrine, a woman isn't allowed to address the congregation from the podium. A JW woman must submit to her husband's "headship," which, like anybody's set of decisions, can be riddled with mistakes and missteps, but like those of the Governing Body, cannot be questioned. "I don't know how I'm supposed to behave," writes Ali Millar in *The Last Days*. "Fortunately, Marc keeps me right and tells me when I've behaved wrongly, or embarrassingly, in public. He tells me to smile if I'm crying, helps me choose the right clothes to wear so I look like a good, loyal sister."

If a woman leaves her Christian husband or if he falls out of *the truth*, she is said to be a *spiritual widow* and becomes a pitiable thing. Abortion is an offence that could lead to a judicial committee hearing, but bearing children can be life-threatening because of the ban on blood transfusions. In this Kingdom of men, the misogyny is complete. This hierarchy works only in a world where trans, nonbinary, and other gender nonconforming people couldn't possibly exist.

My baby sister, Catrina, was only six months old when the massacre at École Polytechnique—the anti-feminist killing of fourteen women—occurred mere kilometres from our home. I was thirteen at the time and happy to assume a role that was more parent than sibling, even if I did spoon as much puréed mango baby food into my mouth as I did hers. But the darkness that December was total; it never got brighter, even on days it didn't snow. In the following weeks and months, I feared for the little sister in my care and for the world she would grow to inherit. I wouldn't always be there to protect her, to read to her from Peter Rabbit picture books as if nothing else existed. It would be years before I learned that the Kingdom Hall we attended wasn't as interested in her safety as I was, and that the literature we studied taught the hatred of women.

Congregations are organized around personal loyalties to powerful men, as each worshipper seeks to increase their standing in the fold by aligning themselves with the strongest. Question the decisions of the higher-ups, no matter how arbitrary, and they will accuse you of apostasy and a lack of faith, which are grounds for shunning—a tool of the patriarchy. The shunned person, despite being outcast and stripped of all power, is called an abuser for daring to criticize God's supposedly perfect Word as interpreted through the elders. Apostates are evil and cannot be trusted to tell their stories, so the congregation never hears their side. A sick reversal takes place: apostates are cast as the ones doing the shunning, since they're *turning their backs on Jehovah*.

"In our own realms—families, cliques, communities, workplaces—we have all experienced the patriarch, the male supremacist, the nationalist, the racist or just the local provincial big man who will not tolerate any opposition," writes Sarah Schulman in *Conflict Is Not Abuse: Overstating Harm, Community Responsibility, and the Duty of Repair*. This is the type of person who won't seek resolution if it means admitting he might be wrong, because it would be unthinkable for him to apologize. He may feel that to get any support at all he must claim total victimhood, that even participating in discussion or negotiation—availing himself to power of any kind—is to waive his right to help.

This behaviour then radiates outward. "He expects that once he asserts his position, everyone else will obey, fall in line, and that this is how the moment is resolved: through obedience." Out of a misplaced sense of loyalty, friends join him in shunning the person who challenged him, as if that's what being a friend means. This new group may use the law to punish an already marginalized individual, which creates far more harm than the discomfort they were looking to avoid.

In these examples, Schulman is *not* referring to cases of stalking, harassment, intimate partner violence, or other types of abuse and boundary crossing, where cutting off contact is often a necessity. Communities have the right to protect themselves and each other, which includes de-platforming abusers, an idea Schulman supports by the very fact of writing about the "culture of under-reaction to abuse and overreaction to conflict," the latter making it more difficult to identify abuse when it happens.

Years ago, Arsenal Pulp Press contacted me to provide reader notes on *Conflict Is Not Abuse*, which they were considering for publication. I took detailed notes on the text and thought I understood it. Still, it has taken me years to realize how much the book narrates my personal experience. Now, when I read about how "shunning is not only a punitive silencing, but it is a removal from humanity, and therefore reliant on the Making of Monsters," I become aware of the irony of applying this to the JW context. If the JWs consider themselves *already* removed from humanity, doesn't kicking someone out of the group *rejoin* the person to society? When Schulman writes about how this expulsion "has no terms for resolution, it is simply a form of asserting supremacy and imposing punishment, and punishment, as we know, rarely does anything but produce more pain," she transports me to the two funerals I attended for old congregation friends who'd died of substance abuse that now, in retrospect, I see is so obviously connected to their being outcast.

I've always minimized how I was shunned, using a million excuses. When I moved from the Montreal suburbs to downtown, I would probably have lost contact with my community anyway. Here's another one: *I* am the one shunning *them*. After all, I'm the one who left. But these thoughts are distortions. The shunning I experienced was real. It's possible that, when I saw members of my former congregation turn away from me in the street, I didn't notice right away because I was intoxicated by the wonders of my new— if more solitary—life. It's possible that I've downplayed my shunning for years because I don't want to acknowledge the pain it has caused me, for then I would be responsible for it and would have to start healing somehow, which is hard work.

Eventually, I took it the other way. The new narrative I started telling myself was that my shunning was total, that I'd been forcibly separated from almost everyone I'd known for the first two decades of my life. But the more I thought about my experiences, and the more I remembered them, I began to realize that this wasn't exactly true. So where was the balance? Where in the middle ground did the truth lie?

The key for me was to recognize that I was using an oversimplified definition of the word *departure*. Many in the ex-JW community use a set of acronyms to identify where on the departure spectrum someone is: PIMI (physically in, mentally in), PIMO (physically in, mentally out), POMI (physically out, mentally in), and POMO (physically out, mentally out). In the case of PIMOs, who must remain undercover— living outwardly as obedient Jehovah's Witnesses without revealing their doubts to the congregation—having a way to signal their status in the online ex-JW community can be crucial for their personal safety. These acronyms are correct in implying that departing anything is a process, but they can also lead to oversimplification. At times, the stops on this journey are portrayed to be unidirectional. For some leaving high-control groups, the *once you're out, you're out* stance provides a kind of certainty that feels helpful. It's easier to forge a new life if you can point to a sharp line separating you from your old one. I realize why it could be uncomfortable to admit that leaving the Watch Tower can be a lifelong project—it might discourage some from leaving at all.

But in my experience, departing *anything* is a lifelong goodbye. For many queers, "coming out" has meant doing it dozens of times for dozens of audiences, in ways that are forever new. So it follows that my original letter of disassociation was simply a template. There would be no end to the breakup letters I'd have to write, because Jehovah can hold onto pieces of you long after you leave. To name just one example, it took over a decade after renouncing the Jehovah's Witnesses for what I called my "Armageddon clouds" to go away, for me to stop fully believing I would die along with almost everyone I knew at the end of days. In *Interior States*, Meghan O'Gieblyn writes that "to be a former believer is to perpetually return to the scene of the crime," and I feel that statement in my very bones.

Of course, not all ex-JWs define *in* and *out* so clearly; it's ultimately impossible to do so. How someone fades in or out of the religion might take an unrecognizable shape. They could shift between being PIMQ and POMQ (physically in or out, and mentally questioning): acronyms with just enough nuance to describe the liminal and skirt the binaries that replicate modes of JW thinking.

———

Despite what the Witnesses claim, they don't make the question of *in* or *out* easy. When I disassociated, I indeed lost contact with most of the people I knew. By this, I mean the hundred or so fellow congregants I grew up with: my friends and their families. Sometimes the grandparents knew my grandparents from way back. I lost touch with Natalya, who'd been a key part of my friend crew. I'd been close to Paul, her cousin, who was our Kingdom Hall's other stutterer. We'd bonded over the ways our speech set us apart, how different the Kingdom vocabulary sounded when it came out of our mouths, how we would receive the same cure in the *new system*. It felt doubly cruel when Paul no longer wanted to hang out with me, but I didn't blame him. He was simply in a group that forced him to stutter alone.

There was Cyrus, who used to have me over to his house every summer for pool parties. I'd look up his trunks surreptitiously, then try not to think about his hairy, dangling cock when we played Battleship together. I have a photo of the two of us graduating high school together, arms thrown over each other's shoulders, a show of familiarity and love, and for me, desire. Our communication stopped the day my letter of disassociation was read aloud at the hall. I heard that Cyrus later declared himself part of the Anointed Class, one of the 144,000 Witnesses called to heaven, as opposed to most JWs, who are doomed to live forever on earth. I wonder if I played a part in scaring him into his heavenly calling.

There was Stephen, who'd moved from the West Coast to Montreal and whose sense of humour I shared. Born goofs, we'd joke in field service and at the meetings. Stephen was tall and reddish blond and had the most infectious laugh. He was in his twenties when I was in my teens, and I looked up to him for the example he set: clean-cut, hard-working, devoted to serving Jehovah. He became a ministerial servant not long after joining our congregation, and he was no doubt destined to become an elder and reach other heights. It made sense that after I left I could no longer talk to him. It would be years before I discovered what havoc Stephen's own shunning would create in his life.

Others, if I ran into them in public, averted their eyes and otherwise pretended I didn't exist. Two of my aunts shunned me, which cut me off from five of my Florida cousins for years—including one who was named after me but whom I'd never met. It was easy for the congregation to spin the narrative that I'd brought this upon myself. After all, on paper, I *chose* to leave, as if I had a choice to remain after what I'd disclosed about myself to the elder on the phone that queer evening. After I'd sent my letter the congregation never formally checked in to see how I was doing, which you'd think they'd do if the group's policies were supposedly founded on love, or, at the very least, if they saw me as an investment they could one day recoup, which they're still trying to do.

What was less clear-cut, however, was how each Witness applied the command to shun. I now understand that everyone does it differently. Some of the people who *should've* shunned me didn't. I continued to live with my mom and stepdad for another year and a half. When an adult who has removed themselves from God's grace still lives at home, a parent is allowed to speak to them about the mundane, functional things of life, but they can't engage in anything deeper together, such as spiritual matters. If we were silent around the dinner table, it wasn't in observance of the rules; our household tension was simply too great. Nothing changed between my stepdad and me, except maybe he felt more solidarity with me now that I was out of the religion. He'd also stopped going to meetings by that point, leaving my mom as the only sucker in the house destined to live forever, which must've made her feel lonely. My stepdad didn't outwardly object to her remaining a JW, and neither did I; I would only articulate that objection much later. Catrina was too young to have made a stand.

Later, after I moved away, my mom never shunned me, even though not to do so was against the rules. I'm extremely grateful to her for this, and for how she preserved my ability to stay connected to my sister. Catrina remains part of the bedrock of my life. Thank God *the truth* never took with her, even though she attended meetings and book study growing up, just as I did. It's interesting how this happens with siblings across many religious groups, how it sticks with one and not the other. I admire this gene of resistance in her.

Some Witnesses acknowledged me in public—such as at the grocery store—as an act of basic human decency, and pretended that nothing was wrong, but invitations to their parties and other events dried up. And some friends didn't care because they were on their own way out of the organization. There was Ian, for example, who loved to party. Although I was the first to formally leave, I suspect that he and my bandmate Danny had gotten a head start on that. In our band Danny was the best musician, and I was jealous of his dark lyrics: evidence of a deep soul, someone who thought for himself. Like Ian, he disappeared into the drug scene, and in his drift, became more himself.

Despite any contact I was able to maintain with the people in my life, I was still lonely and isolated. This was pre-internet, and there was no one I could talk to about being queer. I had the men I slept with, but we didn't talk much. The exceptions to shunning were a relief, but they were also confusing. I suppose that's when I decided to live a life that would force people to act more definitively on the matter of shunning me.

———

Growing up, my best friend wasn't a Jehovah's Witness. My connection to Dave started with note passing at the back of grade nine math class. We recognized the clown in each other, someone worthy of skipping algebra lessons with. We wrote song lyrics together without any intention of setting them to music—a pair of regular Bernie Taupins. Dave was a *worldly* person who had political opinions and was vocal about them.

Dave's songwriting took off when America dropped bunker busters on Kuwait during the Gulf War. It was obvious that the war was a ruse to control oil reserves in the region, that it had nothing to do with freedom. Dave protested imperialism, but for me, the idea of humans achieving freedom without Jehovah was the real offence. For Witnesses, to be free means to be free of *the world*. So, equipped with our separate reasons, Dave and I wrote into the war together.

Dave was a wedge in my belief system by virtue of his very existence. How could Jehovah kill my best friend at Armageddon—this intelligent, handsome, justice-loving individual? Dave changed my opinion of who a *worldly* person could be. He put a face to the evil masses, and to my surprise the face was that of ultimate kindness and under-standing, even if Dave is also the most sarcastic, caustic fuck who ever lived. I never tried to convert him. The idea seems ridiculous. I remember him laughing at titles in the Witness songbook like "Jehovah, Our Best Friend," and I'd have to laugh along with him, which was kind of a fake-it-till-you-disbelieve-it thing for me. I've recently located some of our lyrics. They are perfectly terrible, but we meant everything we wrote.

———

There's a special category of people in my former Jehovah's Witness community that I've only recently become aware of: those who stayed in the group and not only didn't shun me but seemed to encourage me in my worldly ways. They may have even done things to facilitate my departure, not as an act of pushing me out, but maybe to live certain things vicariously through me. In the end, they nurtured the baby apostate in me and are as guilty of it as I am.

After I disassociated, I continued to hang out with my bandmate Myles for another two years. We fed the engine of humour that kept our relationship going; there was always something new to laugh at. Perhaps he liked being part of a band with two spiritual rebels. Myles was the eldest, the clean-living one, the straight-edge guitarist who brought stability to our trio. He was always on time, never missed a jam session, and never swore. I suspect that part of his decision to remain in contact with me and Danny—and especially with me, which was formally disallowed for him— was curiosity about what life looked like on the outside. He could be us in an alternative universe, untethered from Jehovah and free to explore all the sin that lyrics by the bands we listened to promised. So what kind of a Witness *was* Myles? Was he applying the rules correctly, or are there simply as many valid loopholes as there are Jehovah's Witnesses?

Jude was another friend in this category. Tall, and as straight as the spine of a Bible. When we were both young teens, he would invite me over to his room and teach me how to lift weights. I remember the day we chilled on his single mattress and he played "Smells Like Teen Spirit." Nirvana was a sound from another world, not the one of songbooks and Bible bags and meeting shoes. He let the world in me that day, and I think he knew it. I was so taken with the funky smells of his room, that evangelical musk with just a hint of sex. I borrowed his sweaters when it was too cold to walk home without one and would sniff them for weeks.

Once, I went with Jude to a party Ian was throwing, which meant it was an all-nighter. We smoked hash until it stained our hands, and both of us went straight to work without sleep. If Jude was technically still a Witness, how could he sin this hard and not be disciplined for it? Was it simply a matter of his entourage not turning him in? Was it because he was straight? I'm sure I'm missing some backstory; every Witness life is a farm of disconnected siloes. Whatever it was, he found ways to break the rules but remain in *the truth*, to have his Nirvana and listen to it, too.

What's clear is that for many of my friends, the difference between *in* and *out* has been as unclear for them as it has been for me. The binary of good and evil isn't as definitive as the Jehovah's Witnesses need it to be. The JW rules change constantly so that what is forbidden one year might become a matter of conscience the next. This renders shunning, when it occurs, even more tragic; if shunning can never be executed completely across all believers and situations, it cannot be policed and nor can its aims be achieved. It's totally unnecessary.

I think back to those summer days playing Battleship, Cyrus and I hidden from each other behind the plastic grid, calling out shots and trying to guess each other's moves. Just a few pegs in either direction and we could've switched places: he the heathen and me the Anointed, ready for a coronation in the Kingdom of men.

———

You'd think that since I grew up in a group that preaches shunning, I'd be aware of when I was doing it to others. If I've shunned anyone in my post-JW life, it probably wasn't in an obvious way; it was more of a slow freeze, so slow that at first you didn't feel the temperature drop. I'm sure it started when I forgot your birthday, or didn't congratulate you on a new job, book, or breakthrough. We might've had a two-year stretch when I'd answered your emails right away, then suddenly I pushed that to a week, a month, three months. I probably did it for the same reason some Jehovah's Witnesses do it: I recognized a part of myself in you I was afraid to grasp and didn't want to see. A noticeable gap opened between us. Maybe you could no longer feel your place in the fibre of my growth. I know not all delays are an act of shunning, but still. I never meant to ghost you. I didn't know silence could hurt that much, but I should have. Every day we have infinite ways to inflict violence on one another, to alter mental health for the worse. There's more I could've done to prevent it from happening. This is not an excuse. None of this is okay.

Sometimes, my avoidance of people appears to be rooted in internalized homophobia. Growing up, I figured out there was something different about my mom's cousin Louise by how the family said her name, as though she were a danger-ous character. Later, I would learn that Lulu—as I called her—was the first out queer in the family. She was butch and outspoken and didn't take shit from anybody. At sixteen she threw on a baseball cap and sneaked into Chez Jilly's, a Montreal lesbian bar that was raided in 1976, the year I was born, as part of a pre-Olympics morality sweep. Lulu was never in the Jehovah's Witnesses, yet she still had to contend with conservative family values and all that they legislated.

By the time I was in my thirties, she and I had bumped into each other only once or twice a decade, usually at family gatherings. She told me about her job as a social worker and always gave me a bear hug. She was probably one of the safest people for me to come out to, but I never did. Year after year, when I updated her about my life, I sidestepped any talk of sexuality or partners. Maybe I was afraid of the power we'd create by publicly acknowledging each other—a queer nucleus that could blow up the family, even though every year, fewer within it remained Jehovah's Witnesses.

At a funeral Lulu and I both attended, I had had enough. I was sick of missed opportunities to connect, to acknowledge a lineage of resistance. I came out to her mere feet from the open casket, and in a fit of joy she threw her arms around me and said "Welcome to the family!" When I told her about the queer life I'd lived, her mood shifted. "Why am I finding out only now?" It was my fault, and I had no justification. Had I come out to her long before, I could have reduced her isolation, and mine. I was already out to most of the family. I would've asked her to take me to the building where Chez Jilly's once stood, to show me the secret back door behind which she nursed her Coke, because the bar knew, of course, that a raid was coming. But she was mostly angry at the family. "Why couldn't they tell me the truth about you?" I suspect my queerness was something they thought they should keep quiet about. Maybe they were afraid of our power together, as I had been. Together, Lulu and I would be unstoppable, and now we're left making up for the time we spent as two queers bumbling in our own corners of the family, a nucleus separated into particles in search of the other.

WE WILL ALL BE IN FLORIDA SOON

In 2014, when I was thirty-eight, my maternal grandmother was dying of chronic COPD, a debilitating lung condition, and had only a few months to live. I flew to St. Petersburg, Florida, where she had retired with my grandfather, to see her one last time. My mom and I flew separately because we couldn't get tickets on the same flight. I rented a sports car at the airport and crossed the W. Howard Frankland Bridge, wondering if I'd ever see dolphins breach in Old Tampa Bay again. In that drive over the miles of asphalt mere feet above the expanse of warm gulf waters, I felt I was in a movie version of my life. I cranked up 80s soft rock on the radio and carelessly blasted the air conditioning so that it spilled out the open sunroof. I wanted to feel everything at once, to relive and to let go.

My mom arrived in St. Pete before I did. I picked her up at my aunt Joanne's house and drove her to the little roadside motel I'd booked for us. My mom's relationship with her parents is complicated and not my story to tell. I knew the visit would be tough for her, and I wanted to be a good support. She, in turn, wanted me to say my goodbyes to Grandma and form my final memories of her. My mother believed in closure and wanted me to have it. She and I hadn't taken a mother-son trip since I was a kid. This was a new phase of our relationship, where we were no longer only parent and child, but also adult friends.

Maybe we were more like teens. We hopscotched across six lanes of traffic for midnight trips to the nearby Walmart, risking our lives for the cheapest junk food on the planet and to browse items we had no intention of buying. We acted like spring breakers when we hit the white sand beaches not far from the iconic Don CeSar hotel, a.k.a. the Pink Castle, where we cavorted in our swimsuits and took selfies. She and I are seventeen years apart; people often mistake us for siblings, and sometimes, other things. It was one of the most beautiful weeks my mother and I have ever spent together.

On the drive to Grandma Dee's, my mother warned me not to be shocked by her physical condition. The disease had emaciated Dee to the point where she was a husk of herself.

She had sunken cheeks and a protruding skull, and no longer ate solid food. But I wasn't shocked—I could still see Grandma in there, her trademark snark, the air of a 1940s movie star.

Baseball was our way of saying goodbye together; it was something we'd always shared. I sat beside her on the sofa while she sucked on a cherry ice pop for the carbs and we watched her precious Rays kick the shit out of a lesser team whom she badmouthed. In that way, she hadn't changed a bit. "Come on, throw the ball, you stupid bums." Yes, the real Dee lived in the way she could throw shade, in the withering looks she gave my grandfather when he spoke and otherwise interrupted her baseball time, the looks that made him leave the room.

From birth until around the age of four, I lived with my mom and her five siblings at my grandparents' house (options were limited for a single mom and her kid in the 1970s). Grandma Dee and I had a special bond that seemed to revolve around a baseball diamond. We watched Montreal Expos catcher Gary Carter pick off runners at second base while she did the laundry or made ice cream sandwiches. Word was that before she met my grandfather she'd go to Montreal Royals games with her sisters and flirt from the stands with a certain second baseman, who would wink at her. (I would have preferred a professional baseball player to a professional Jehovah's Witness for a grandfather any day.) The former site of Delorimier Stadium now sits three and a half blocks away from a Kingdom Hall, which is a great metaphor for my grandmother—forever adjacent to Jehovah. Maybe the promise of being close to the West Palm Beach Expos, a Montreal farm team, had made moving so far from home more bearable for her.

Seeing Grandma with COPD wasn't as shocking as the treatment I received from my mother's sister Joanne, who had once shown me love until it proved to be conditional. She was one of the women who helped raise me, alongside my mom. When I was a kid, Joanne and I would go horseback riding, back when there were stables in the West Island. Later, after she'd moved to Florida and on my visits there, she took me to Disney World, Sunken Gardens, Busch Gardens, and nearly every other theme park where I could play with dangerous wildlife I wasn't already in contact with.

But now that I was disassociated, everything had changed. I spent hours in Grandma Dee's house with my aunt Joanne, and she couldn't even bring herself to meet my eye. It's painful when someone you've known your entire life stares right past you that way, walks through you as if you're a ghost. I recently found the last letter Joanne ever wrote to me. It's brimming with love. This is curious, because according to the date on the letter she'd sent it *after* I'd disassociated from the group, which suggests that my mom had delayed telling her about my departure.

"Why don't you go outside with your grandfather?" my mother asked when the ball game was over. The idea was for the two of us to share our final moments together; it was obvious that he didn't have much time left, either.

I knew what would happen as soon as we stepped outside.

———

For me, the trip represented the end of an era in my childhood. I'd visited Florida every summer from the time I was about eight until I was sixteen. My mom, my stepdad, and I would drive there like typical Canadian snowbirds, stopping for peaches, fireworks, and empty novelty cans of "Florida Sunshine" on our way down the eastern seaboard. Sometimes I flew with my mother, and once I flew alone as an unaccompanied minor, having to wear a sticker that the flight attendants and other airline staff could recognize me by.

Joanne and her husband, Gary, once paid for my ticket in exchange for a summer of yard work (which has since made me question my immediate family's socio-economic status within the larger family). My daily chores consisted of fishing the turtles and snakes out of the in-ground pool, mowing the lawn, cutting the elephant ears, picking bananas, limes, oranges, and grapefruit, and whacking weeds I knew would grow back by the next morning. Things grow five times faster in the thick Florida humidity than they do anywhere else. I smelled permanently of lawn-mower gas. My mom once had to negotiate with my elementary school teachers so that I could do a few months of coursework from Florida.

I was the ringleader among my younger Floridian cousins. We pretended to pilot a pleasure craft that sat idly in my aunt and uncle's yard, several miles from the Gulf of Mexico. With another one of my uncles, I built a raft out of a wood pallet and four empty five-gallon paint drums that served as pontoons. I'd sail onto the lagoon across from the house with Donna, the geriatric family dog, in search of adventure. There was a rumour that neighbours had released an unwanted pet python into the wetlands, one that had grown over the years into a creature big enough to take down a kid or a dog. Picture a marine remake of *The Littlest Hobo* meets *The Love Boat* meets *Anaconda*. The resident parrots Sam and Bozo could speak and did so prolifically.

They called Donna's name from shore just to make her crazy; the dog never knew who was calling her.

On drives across the state along Interstate 75, I dreamt of scaling the twelve-foot fences topped with barbed wire so that I could luxuriate in the Everglades mud with the gators and contemplate the blue, blue sky. I had less affinity for the swan that attacked me when my foot was caught in what I believed was quicksand on a golf course I never should have been on in the first place. That's the thing about Florida: you don't have to go to a nature preserve to commune with wildlife; it's everywhere. Turtles crossed the road like lethal speed bumps. And you couldn't exactly relax at Treasure Island sandcastle-building competitions amid the ever-present threat of shark attacks.

Florida dogs are particularly fearsome, or at least that was my perspective as a bite-sized Jehovah's Witness coming unbidden up walkways with my aunt Joanne. Floridians are obsessed with the concepts of personal property and trespassing. Some of them hated it when you not only dared enter their palatial estates flanked by palms and dotted with temperature-controlled swimming pools but then asked if they'd like to live in Paradise—as if they didn't already. People could be as vitriolic as their attack dogs, barking out that we had no right to be there, that we were violating bylaws, that we were delusional. If I'd only known how right they were I could have extracted myself from the whole charade sooner. I might have chased myself back down the walkway and soaked my *Watchtower* magazines in the nearest lagoon. Who knew enlightenment had been available to me in America's reddest state?

The highlight of my Florida trips was always Grandma Dee. She knew the kind of places where I needed to take refuge. I chased lizards and whacked golf balls into the creek behind her house, which, at the time, flowed strong and almost reached the top of the retaining wall. She took me to Pass-a-Grille Beach where I threaded live shrimp on hooks and fished for bottom feeders while she tanned nearby. We could spend hours in silence together. She let me browse the local pawnshops where I drooled over guitar amplifiers too big to take back to Montreal. The reward for not breaking my neck my first time go-carting was peanut butter and chocolate ice cream, the kind of hybrid I could only dream about in Canada in the 1980s. Happiness could sometimes be so simple.

At the centre of me sits a Florida lagoon—no, an Everglades of unlimited scope. Or quicksand in which both my feet are permanently stuck. I revisit the Florida of my mind when I want to feel both grounded and detached.

Some days I pretend I did all my growing up there. I have never left the raft, and the raft has never stopped wobbling. I have made it to the other side of the fence along the I-75 and nestled with the gators into the mud of memory. There are parts of me I should have let the reptiles strangle and there are parts I should have let germinate a little longer in the loam. Each of my eight summers in Florida feels like a generation, an opportunity to have reinvented my world. Missed opportunities sit at the bottom of the pool, the lagoon, the gulf, and I can only speculate how big they might have grown over time.

If the coastline of Florida is of no fixed shape and constantly shifts in my mind, it does so in real life as well. We cannot talk about Florida without talking about climate crisis. I've never lived through a hurricane there, but I've arrived in the aftermath and heard the stories about family boarding up and battening down. I've seen entire Panhandle news cycles devoted to the panic that an early frost induces, what it does to the flesh of an orange, to the morale of a citrus farmer. Maybe Mario Alejandro Ariza is right when he writes that "if you expect to survive into the middle of the twenty-first century, you just might get to watch Miami die."

When I was growing up, the dream of Florida was real. It was a soft sell; snowbirds fell hard for it. Now I don't have to leave Montreal to feel the same heat or humidity. As the earth overheats and turns into a scorched, fiery wasteland, the Florida heat I long for so nostalgically will follow me wherever I go. We will all be in Florida soon.

———

Unlike with Grandma Dee, I hadn't been prepared to see the extent of Grandpa Keith's physical deterioration. He was completely hunched over, his smile and teeth warped by time. He had survived prostate cancer and was in his nineties. He shuffled his walker onto the lawn that had become so bald that it was now half St. Augustine grass and half sand. We walked to the spot overlooking the creek, which was now practically dry; I could see every rock on its bed. Climate change was ravaging Florida. I worried for the wetlands, the marshes, the gators. I worried for Florida.

It's worth noting that Keith is the one who got us into this mess. I'm told that he and his brother joined the Jehovah's Witnesses and pretended to be members to avoid having to serve in World War II. What I don't understand about this narrative is how he expected to get better treatment as a Witness. The Canadian government outlawed the group under the War Measures Act between 1940 and 1943 while

I wondered if they were taking a jab at the soggy convention sandwiches we got for free. Just then, my grandfather, one of the complainers, fell to the stage and clutched his shin. Bitten by an invisible serpent! That should teach him a lesson for disbelieving in Jehovah. He was instructed to stare at a replica of a venomous snake on a pole that Moses had made—the only way to survive the bite, the venom of one's own wavering faith.

Replace the snake on a pole with Jesus on the cross, and you have a prediction of Christianity thousands of years before it happened, illuminated on a sun-splashed platform near where second base normally was. Swap the Old Testament version of my grandfather with the 1980s model, and I have a Moses stand-in that I could be punished for disobeying. I was supposed to be grateful for what Keith had been through, since it was for our benefit. He'd done time for Jehovah, which had purchased our family a higher standing in the ranks of the Witnesses, whether this had been his intention or not. It felt like we owed him something. It would've been difficult—or impossible—for my mother, raising a child on her own and living with my grandparents and her siblings, *not* to stick to the Jehovah program. Her skipping meetings would've been a betrayal of my grandfather's experience, just as how my departure was a betrayal of what my mother had risked when she refused a blood transfusion.

Jesus, my mother, my grandfather. They're all very different people to me, yet they all held the power to redeem me if only I were grateful, humble, obedient enough.

I felt little affection for Keith. He did terrible things that created generations of trauma in our family. The fact that he appeared to follow the moral guidelines of a religious group helped to hide it. There in the backyard, standing beside him, the breeze blew through the Spanish moss hanging from the trees overhead.

"Danny, have you thought about your relationship to Jehovah?"

"Thanks, I'll think about that if I'm ever ready."

"Remember our heavenly father is a forgiving one, and he is always ready to welcome us back."

I copped out of having a real conversation with my grandfather, possibly the only one we would ever have, because I didn't see the point in confronting him over religion. We were firmly on different sides of the creek, and nothing would change that. When he died, the scrub would grow over the house and overtake it, along with the lizards. I just wanted to enjoy the serenity of one of my childhood homes before I would lose it forever, before my family would renovate it and sell it to another family who would soon make their own memories there. I should have told him to go fuck himself. Why had I chickened out? Where was my rage at what he'd done to this family?

Keith preached to the very end, blocking the sidewalks of St. Pete with his mobility scooter to snag passersby. As a Witness who died while practising, he qualifies for what is called the Resurrection; the dead will literally come to life in a utopia. But where will he be resurrected *to*? A Florida whose temperature melts human skin? Most importantly, *who* will he be resurrected to? His cellmates? Duplessis? Most of my family—except for my mother, my aunt Joanne, two other aunts through marriage, and a second cousin—have left *the truth*. Those who leave have no chance of resurrection, according to some interpretations of the doctrine, which seems to be ever-changing.

Keith could very well awaken alone on a sidewalk in St. Pete.

He got us into this mess, and he will have to get himself out of it.

———

When I was living in New York in my twenties, I booked a seat to Tampa on a discount airline that lost my bag, but

I didn't care because I was going to see Grandma Dee. I knew better than to expect my aunt Joanne to let me into her house. By then she knew I was a diseased apostate.

Like my mom, Grandma didn't shun me. She accepted and loved me for who I was. She didn't make a practice of shunning anyone, least of all her family. Humans were always more important to her than doctrine. As far as I could tell, she didn't attend JW meetings often, but the family pretended she did. She tolerated my grandfather's religious zeal and outwardly went along with it. I never saw her preach door to door, probably because of the stutter she and I share. If she ever stopped believing, it would be easier for her to coast along this way than to face the social rupture that results from expressing doubts.

It has occurred to me that my mother has probably modelled her version of being a JW on Grandma: a toe in when it's convenient, interpreting certain rules creatively, ignoring the ones that are inhumane. I was raised by loving women for whom shunning doesn't come naturally, and who, when asked to do it, refuse. It has also occurred to me that maybe they're the reason I've never considered being a Jehovah's Witness a binary.

My mother disputes this interpretation. She says that her reason for not shunning me is that I was "just a baby" when

I got baptized at thirteen and when I left at eighteen, barely old enough to know what I was doing in either case. Furthermore, I couldn't have learned anything since then, least of all gained any insight into Jehovah's Witnesses, because wisdom can come only from Jehovah. In her view, my brain is frozen in 1994 and unable to compute anything new, and I remain "a spiritual minor." Whether she sees me as a baby or as barely human, I lack the agency to have broken the rules in a way that merits shunning. What an elaborate scheme to evade what I feel is the real reason: deep down, she believes that shunning is cruel and she couldn't possibly do it to one of her children.

I'm sure Grandma had her own moments of zeal, those sudden pangs of fear the Society cultivates so well in its members. She sent a letter to me the year before I flew from New York to visit her. "I guess you know your Mom told me you disassociated yourself from the congregation. It was very distressful news to us, and I know your Mom is devastated, too . . . Whatever the problem, please don't let family or friends influence you in any way. You know our future happiness only comes from God. Jehovah is always there for us like a close friend . . . We wouldn't want to find ourselves on the 'outside' when we know the time is getting nearer for this system to end." When she got to the part about my being "an inspiration to us all," the horror of a new question bloomed in me: Had *I* been the Super Witness in the family all these years, with everyone following *my* example? But when we were together, Grandma Dee spoke to me quite differently. This kind of cognitive dissonance—of living in multiple realities at once—is very common among Jehovah's Witnesses.

Even though I was then an adult, Grandma indulged me the same way she always had. She made me her famous date squares and molasses cookies and took me fishing. I could still bait a live shrimp, though I'd grown worse at actually catching anything. She pretended not to notice as she worked on her tan. One such time, casting for catfish, I grew itchy and asked her to take me home. I thought it was the salty brine that was irritating my skin and that a shower would fix it. I combed through my chest hair in the bathroom and saw legs wriggling in protest. The worst had happened, and I had to tell her.

"Grandma, I think I have crabs."

"Let's go to the pharmacy," she said without missing a beat, as if she'd done this before.

I picked up a bottle of Nix, and on the way back we made a plan: shampoo myself with the treatment, wash all the bedding, clean the upholstery, vacuum the rugs, and keep the news from my grandfather. It was special to vacuum her house of my crabs together, one of the most intimate things I've experienced with anybody. I saw corners of her life I never knew existed. Grandma knew where crabs came from—she wasn't naive. They weren't your typical Florida critters. I had obviously imported them from New York as creatures of sin, yet she never let me feel that I'd lost my innocence as the decades rolled by.

There's a photo I have of Dee and I playing cards at her dining room table when I was much younger, the sun streaming in through the patio door behind us. There would be a winner and a loser—simply the rules of the game. I'm looking past my cards and through Dee at something I recognized: we were both Tampa Bay sharks. Two of a kind.

THE WITNESS IS COMPLICIT

Jehovah's Witnesses drive by my place in suvs, creeping up and down the block all weekend. I hide behind the blinds to do them a favour; I'm an apostate, dangerous to their faith. A single word from my mouth could poison their minds and jeopardize their chances of living forever.

It turns out they don't care if no one seems to be home. They ring anyway. I open the door to an adult and a teen asking me if I know who they are. Do they know who *I* am? Can't they see the mark of the beast on my forehead? By this point I've been out of the group for as long as I was *in*. That makes me a dinosaur in apostate years. The teen, who's perhaps around the age I was when I stopped going door to door, seems removed, and might've already mentally checked out of the religion. The pair show me a video on a tablet about the end of the world, as if mine hadn't already ended many times over. I suffer through the video because I'm curious how the JW pitch has evolved over the years. While the delivery is different, the message hasn't changed that much.

The Witnesses are experts at making doomsday come alive in their videos, books, and magazines; their Armageddon branding is ridiculously on point. Famine, one of the Four Horsemen in the Book of Revelation, is a gaunt figure that is hunger personified. Tornadoes, hurricanes, and earthquakes rip the earth apart like an orange. Natural disasters were always a sign of the times, but now the literature can use climate devastation to proclaim even more forcefully that the end is near. Inevitably, a figure emerges from the blood-red sky on a white horse and brandishing a sword: Jesus, authorized by his father, Jehovah God, topples buildings onto the wicked and they die by the billions. He sweeps the rubble and corpses into a gaping abyss that yawns plumes of sulphur dioxide. He crushes entire militaries with a pinky.

We interpreted these warnings literally. Whenever the skies darkened and a storm loomed, whispers of Armageddon were not far off. News of an earthquake always led to Witnesses at the hall shrugging at one another with it's-the-time-of-the-end looks. You'd think the threat of cataclysmic natural disaster would provoke fear, but strangely, the idea made us calm. For Witnesses, the disintegration of the earth's crust would be a *good* development, a precursor to a new world; such an implosion would be better than spending one more minute with evildoers. And when all this horror finally takes place, the faithful are supposed to just hide in safehouses and wait it out.

The Witnesses have long maintained that pestilence will be a sign of the Last Days. Death, another one of the Four Horsemen, is a skeleton that rides hard, spreading disease and reaping lives. Unsurprisingly, the Witness book *Revelation—Its Grand Climax At Hand!* finds a way to moralize about virus transmission. "In what was described as 'the ugly decade' of the 1980s, a way of life that is lawless by Bible standards added the scourge of AIDS to the 'deadly plague.'"

This kind of fearmongering couldn't stop me from leaving the cult; rather, it made me eager to become the kind of sexual outlaw they shun. I joined a queer community that took care of one another during a plague and that religion had already left for dead. Revelling in the touch and warmth of queer and hated bodies would indeed mark the first time I felt that a new world was actually possible.

How much of this do I tell the two at my door? Should I say I'm writing a book about them and the colours of the Armageddon sky?

———

The Watchtower predicted Armageddon would come in 1925. That year, Sears, Roebuck & Company started selling the Thompson submachine gun. The Tri-State Tornado killed almost seven hundred people. Mussolini gave a speech that would echo far beyond the Italian Chamber of Deputies. The first Surrealist group exhibition opened in Paris on a Friday at midnight—Miró's work warping the social order while the bourgeoisie slept. Nellie Tayloe Ross of Wyoming became governor, the first woman to do so, which surely spelled the end of the world for someone.

In 1929, Judge Rutherford, then president of the Watch Tower Society, built Beth Sarim, a ten-room villa in San Diego. According to the deed, the house was to be kept in trust for the "princes" of the Old Testament, for when they would be resurrected. Rutherford planted trees and shrubs native to Bible lands so that these reanimated men could recognize their new home. Someone else obviously now owns the house, but it still awaits its intended occupants.

The Witnesses also believed that the end would come in 1975. At a 1967 district convention in Sheboygan, Wisconsin, attendees were told to "stay alive to seventy-five." The March 1968 issue of *Our Kingdom Ministry* says, "Just think, brothers, there are only about ninety months left before 6,000 years of man's existence on earth is completed. Do you remember what we learned at the assemblies last summer? The majority of people living today will probably be alive when Armageddon breaks out, and there are no resurrection hopes for those who are destroyed then."

As 1975 approached, the Society grew afraid of the repercussions of getting it wrong again. Every failed prophecy had so far led to a schism in the group's hierarchy, a hemorrhage in the enrolment numbers, and some form of public shaming. They stopped referring to 1975 overtly, instead resorting to code. At a convention in Los Angeles in February of that year, President Frederick Franz said, "We know it's a critical year. We know we're near *something*. But we're not saying [what]." The crowd laughed and applauded the inside joke.

Many in that crowd would go on to sell their homes and businesses, pass up job opportunities, cash in life insurance policies, drop out of school, and start preaching full time—there was nothing left to lose. But the year passed quietly, and the Society deflected blame. "It may be that some who have been serving God have planned their lives according to a mistaken view of just what was to happen on a certain date or in a certain year . . . If anyone has been disappointed through not following this line of thought, he should now concentrate on adjusting his viewpoint, seeing that it was not the word of God that failed or deceived him and brought disappointment, but that his own understanding was based on wrong premises."

This text is a master class in gaslighting. Only the followers can get it wrong—never the invisible Jehovah. Whenever the Watch Tower messes up a prediction, they cite Proverbs 4:18: "The path of the righteous is like the bright morning light that grows brighter and brighter until full daylight." Because Jehovah reveals *the truth* in degrees, it's normal if the organization gets Armageddon's date wrong a few times.

Thousands of people left the group or were expelled for lacking faith. The Society stopped talking about the 1975 prediction as if it had never happened, and scrubbed references to it in reprints of older publications. (These older books are regularly mass-shredded and deleted from JW.org, which frees the writers of all accountability and leaves past and present members with no trace of the texts that indoctrinated them.) The Society offered fleeting apologies five years later, but the apologies could not give back the years lost to preparing for apocalypse, let alone undo the trauma or sense of dread that can live with a Witness long after they leave.

To many in fundamentalist movements, apocalypse is incremental in its approach. World events, and all the negativity they bring, accumulate to form a picture of The End that grows more plausible every year. The Doomsday Clock ticks forward, never backward. By all accounts, twenty-first-century history supports this. The result is that when I hear about how quickly the ice shelves are melting, or which cities are becoming unlivable due to heat, or which species will go extinct before we can fully document them, I'm afraid of tuning it all out because I was raised in a group that flagged these as signs of an apocalypse I know *not* to be true. Former Jehovah's Witnesses—and others who've left cults or religions— have had to filter out the language of cataclysmic ending when seeking a secular life. We are so inured to the concept that it has become meaningless. To avoid climate passivity, we must redefine Armageddon. We must apply the language of Last Days theology to a new apocalypse that is more horrific than the one we were raised to expect.

The language of climate crisis continues to change at a staggering pace. What do we call our emergencies when we no longer recognize our planet or our place on it? On the need to create environmental warnings for future societies that might use verbal or written patterns unfathomable to us now, Matt Jones writes that "what is interesting about a project designed to communicate ten thousand years in the future is that we think it can be done. That we even try." It's challenging to create new associations for words so that we can restore their urgency. How do we watch the forest fires that decimate the Australian Outback and deteriorate air quality for millions in California and the Pacific Northwest and not compare the situation to tired preconceptions of hell? Fire becomes an abstract idea; symbolism conveniently allows us to avoid thinking about the thing itself.

Nothing earthly, however, can exist in a void of abstraction. To infuse something with new meaning is not to isolate it further, but rather to enliven its web of complicity. Camille T. Dungy solidifies this idea in her essay "Is All Writing Environmental Writing?," in which she outlines the "de-pristining" of her environmental imagination using ecopoetics. "Writing takes off for me when I stop separating human experiences from the realities of the greater-than-human world . . . In a radical and radicalizing way, these fuzzed lines bring me face to face with the fragility of the Holocene—or, more precisely, the destructiveness of the Anthropocene."

I was at work the day my apartment building caught fire. My partner Mark woke up in smoke, ran into the street holding our cat, and called me. I could hear through his sobs that our world had just filled with complicity. We spent the next few months sleeping in the living rooms of friends, surrounded by boxes of clothes we'd salvaged, wrapped in nitrous oxide and the fine particulates of memory. We had no choice but to reduce fire to its elements—the bare truth—and by extension, to redefine our priorities. What was important anymore? Among our remaining possessions was a Poland Spring water bottle that Diamanda Galás left behind at a concert Mark had taken me to. It sparkled near her piano. We grabbed it in case the half ounce of backwash contained her voice.

It took us a while to find a new place. We suspected that a few landlords turned us down because we smelled of smoke, but I was still happy in a way I couldn't explain. For the next year, I lived in the exothermic. I inhaled knowledge about the fire tetrahedron, sniffed books for acceptable levels of smoke damage, and wrote a novel about combustion and queer rights. I tried to make sense of what had happened, and of the miracles of generosity in our friend circle. How had the fire brought me closer to them and transformed my ecosystem? How had it brought me closer to Mark? He made me a mixtape called *Things We Lost in the Fire*, with a track listing I could swear was an inventory of everything we had *found*. It was written in the language of starting over. In time, most of the water in the Poland Spring bottle evaporated. I couldn't understand it. How could anything leave a sealed bottle? "Everything changes," Mark would say, and I would cry.

That year I came to understand fire's raw, destructive power in a way I could never have otherwise. I developed a personal connection to it, and a curiosity that extended to the "greater than human." Now, when I hear about conflagration in the Outback or the Okanagan, I need to know details about the habitats destroyed and the animals threatened. I need to know what cats and wombats do to avoid lung damage. Widening my knowledge can only give me new pathways to empathy.

Meanwhile, the fourth angel from the Book of Revelation pours his bowl upon the sun and scorches us with fire. The rainforest ignites. The ocean acidifies. Coral reefs are bleached from memory. The cryosphere melts. Antarctica and Greenland pass into legend. There is flooding in cities that had never needed seawalls before. The permafrost thaws. Our imaginations widen to horror. At the fifth trumpet blast, smoke ascends from the abyss and darkens the sun. Pipelines gush. The heat dome persists. We open our mouths to protest, but all that comes out is carbon. Unpredictable storms disrupt food production. Many starve, begging for loaves and fishes. The lion lies down with the lamb: they're the only creatures left alive. Millions ridicule Greta Thunberg as they turn to pillars of salt.

———

By early 2020 the Covid-19 pandemic had resuscitated the Society's vision of sickness as portent. Stephen Lett, a member of the Governing Body that controls every aspect of Jehovah's Witness life, spoke to followers about this in a video. "The events unfolding around us are making clear that we're living in the final part of the Last Days, undoubtedly, the final part of the *final part* of the Last Days, shortly before the *Last Day* of the Last Days."

Throughout much of the world, pandemic regulations meant no more knocking on doors. Videoconferences replaced in-person meetings, and the Witnesses learned to conduct Bible studies and shepherding calls remotely. The Society adapted its mostly analog methods to new technology and online publishing replaced much of its print operations, a transition that had already been underway for several years. In September 2020 the Society rolled out the JW Box—a glorified router—to areas where followers don't have reliable internet access. Witnesses could connect to the Box with their phones and download as much *spiritual food* from the doctrine mothership as they liked.

Some in-person activity has resumed at the time of this writing, although many of the online components of worship are here to stay. The Society asks Witnesses to trust the internet and simultaneously tells them it's the most dangerous place to be. They play up fears of apostate hackers and other bad actors. The devil is out there crashing servers and Zoom meetings. It was always understood that sheltering in safe-houses was part of Armageddon, so being stuck in lockdown must've felt like the real thing. Witnesses reached out to past members with we-told-you-so messages, re-exposing them, at an extremely vulnerable moment, to the indoctrination they'd left behind. Now with ongoing worship-from-home, members can permanently inhabit the bunker mentality that is so natural to the group.

Early in the pandemic, I opened the mailbox to find a handwritten letter that starts "DEAR NEIGHBOR, I HOPE THIS LETTER FINDS YOU WELL AND COPING WITH THE CURRENT CRISIS WE ARE ALL FACING," before suggesting

I visit JW.org where I can find "COMFORT FROM THE SCRIPTURES." The letter is written in all caps, but I totally understand—we live in an all-caps era. I can't get over the irony of the closing line: "PLEASE STAY SAFE." For many, staying safe means avoiding Jehovah's Witnesses and their brand of toxicity disguised as kindness. I resisted an initial impulse to shred the letter, and I'm glad I did, because it has since become one of my favourite pandemic mementoes, along with a gym lock whose combination I can no longer remember and tickets to concerts that were never meant to be. The more breakup letters to Jehovah I write, the more letters and postcards from random Jehovah's Witnesses I seem to receive.

When Mark's father died and the family was immersed in grief, his mother received an anonymous letter from a Witness suggesting that her husband was still alive, in the sense that she would see him again in the Resurrection. I wonder how a JW could think it's a good idea to comb funeral notices, sleuth out home addresses, and send these jarring messages, as if they wouldn't only add to trauma.

If the Witnesses were committed to caring about people in a way that mattered, they would mobilize help for their immediate communities instead of preaching to them about an imaginary Paradise where "death and sickness will be no more." They would stop shunning those who've left, those whose isolation is compounded by a pandemic that makes the task of finding new communities more difficult than it already is.

The light doesn't get brighter, but the earth gets hotter. I picture Moses, Ezekiel, and Jeremiah rising from the dead and walking down the San Diego Freeway to Beth Sarim, past forest fires that blanket the area in a thick haze. They will wonder what hell they were resurrected to, and what they did to deserve the punishment of the California sun.

The Witnesses don't ring my bell anymore. I will write the rest of this book without their ministrations, but it will still smell of smoke.

MOONWALKING TO ARMAGEDDON

I crashed a honeymoon when I was eight, in the summer of 1984, when my mom and stepdad took me to Sauble Beach to help celebrate their nuptials. In the daytime I played in the waves of Lake Huron, built sandcastles, and befriended seagulls while my parents tanned. Other families barbecued; frat boys played Frisbee nearby. The water wasn't that deep and there was otherwise nothing to be afraid of, but night-time at our rented cabin was a different story.

On either the first or second night of our stay, a clock kept falling off the wall no matter how many times we put it back up. Same thing with the toilet seat that kept slamming down. It couldn't have been because the cabin was built on sand and was probably tilted, or because that's what toilet seats do. It had to be demons, my mom told me; they swirled through the drafty shack all night, angry that we were Jehovah's Witnesses, determined to convince us of the superiority of evil. My mom sat on my bed and hugged me until morning. She prayed for deliverance and called God's name. *Jehovah, Jehovah, Jehovah.* She was trying to protect me. We left the cabin early, sleepless and before our rental was up, and drove back home to Montreal.

Few outsiders know how keenly aware the JWs are of their own persecution, how they see it as irrefutable evidence that they're on the right path. Whenever a country's government bans their preaching work or shutters Kingdom Halls, members say, "See! They wouldn't do that if we didn't have the truth." When the apparent persecution takes a more paranormal slant, and when it feels as though unseen forces are trying to scare them away from Jehovah—like that night at Sauble Beach—they believe that the Devil and his gang of demons are behind it. It's difficult to explain the logic, and not even the JWs have bothered to work out the details.

Because of all this, the Watch Tower Society constantly warned us not to view the occult as harmless fun, the way it's often portrayed in pop culture. I heard of members getting in trouble for using Ouija boards and otherwise participating in seances, which were reportedly dangerous because they put you in direct contact with demons. We couldn't celebrate birthdays because of their pagan origins and connections to astrology, which the JWs view as a form of divination. On Halloween night we turned off our lights so that we wouldn't be harassed by goblins and witches seeking candy. I wasn't allowed to eat Lucky Charms cereal because shooting stars, green clovers, and horseshoes were "magically delicious," and Witnesses view any form of magic as being inspired by the Devil and antithetical to worshipping Jehovah. The result of this hyperawareness of the occult is that the JWs can appear to be obsessed with it.

The more we were exposed to these surreal beliefs, the more normal they felt. Sometime in 1983, a rumour crept from one Kingdom Hall to another: one Sunday at a Jehovah's Witness meeting—we weren't sure exactly where—a stuffed Smurf allegedly slithered out of a child's lap, shouted obscenities, and walked out of the building. I don't know how this rumour started or how far it spread, but there were suddenly reports that the little blue devils jumped off wallpaper, danced on curtains, and bit kids in their sleep.

The Watchtower told us to destroy anything that showed evidence of possession. Throwing Smurfs into the garbage wasn't enough to make them stop. You had to burn them or rip out the stuffing. I had a Smurfs sing-along record that skipped. It couldn't have had anything to do with the quarter-sized hole in it. I watched, both horrified and grateful, as my uncle smashed it in the backyard with a rock. Around that time, my aunt heard footsteps in the basement of their house and realized the problem was a crystal candy bowl she had inherited from a witchy relative. The story goes that when my uncle tried to smash it, it wouldn't leave his hand.

Maybe the Witnesses were jealous of Smurfs because they live in an exclusive Paradise, the kind of intentional community the JWs dream of. But decades later, I would discover that the Smurf hysteria may not have begun with JWs after all. The fear potentially stemmed from a report about a juvenile gang called "the Smurfs" in Houston, Texas, who, that same year, allegedly assaulted students in bathrooms and murdered a principal. That story turned out to be fabricated—just another extension of the Satanic Panic. Many other evangelical groups had their own demon Smurf stories, so our hysteria was hardly original.

Fear of Satan has always existed in some form or other, but it was brewing in the American consciousness in a new way in the late 1960s, around the time when the Manson Family murdered at least eight people and Anton LaVey founded the Church of Satan. By the 70s *The Exorcist* had entered the public imagination, and by the 80s the Satanic

Panic was in full swing. Police, teachers, parents, therapists, and the Christian fundamentalists among them created a Stranger Danger whisper network that took off. Suddenly, anyone unfamiliar was a threat to children. It was easier to panic about a stranger when a Satanic element was involved. Killer clowns with demonic smiles like serial killer John Wayne Gacy had left a lasting impression; later, following the release of Stephen King's *It*, many other clowns became suspect. On *Unsolved Mysteries*, Robert Stack emerged from the shadows in a trench coat and morgue-like pancake makeup to remind viewers that the spirits were out to get suburban American kids. This was also the era when unfounded reports of Satanic ritual abuse in daycares dominated talk shows and the nightly news.

Where did all this leave me? I was in a group that used its panics to keep members afraid so that they'd stick around for Jehovah's protection. "Beware of Music That Debases!" screamed a 1983 issue of *The Watchtower*, joining the calls of Christian groups worried about sex and demons in rock and metal, even though Witnesses themselves would soon be responsible for producing some of that music.

When the *Awake!* article "Epidemic of Homosexuals" came out that same year, I was too young to understand that it meant *I* could become the feared one, a victim of shunning. I didn't know how easily I could be betrayed by the adults I trusted, and I wasn't supposed to know. We were taught to fear our own minds, to "reject the goal of independent thinking" so that we wouldn't catch on to the group's cultlike manipulations. So, in darkness I continued. Not a single time during the eighteen years I was a member did anyone tell me to watch out for Jehovah and everything being done in that strange ghost's name.

It was the warning I had needed the most.

———

To this day, I'm not sure how many people know that Michael Jackson was the most famous Witness to moonwalk the earth. His religious background—the fact that he and most of his family were JWs—is usually a footnote. I remember a spiral notebook I used for homework that featured Jackson on the cover in a banana-yellow cashmere sweater. He smiled at me conspiratorially. We shared something that no one else at my school did: our fucked-up religion. It's a powerful feeling to be allied with one of the biggest names on the planet that way.

Jehovah's Witnesses aren't supposed to take jobs that place them in the limelight because that would be taking attention away from Jehovah. But once JW stars like Jackson achieved a measure of fame, they entered—unofficially—a category of Witness that was slightly beyond the rules. Maybe their fame could help raise awareness for our message. We were competing with Scientologists and Mormons for superstars, after all, and didn't have a system for developing brand ambassadors as Christian rock did. When we read about the Archangel Michael in the Book of Daniel, and how this Son of God would save humanity, I'm sure some of us read MJ into the text.

Still, the degree to which a famous Jehovah's Witness could rely on their special status was limited. In the 1983 music video *Thriller*, Jackson's werecat eyes, fangs, and claws protrude. Sexual desire teases out the mutation, the beast, and a B-movie cast of zombies flood the street where they ooze into a choreographed number. The elders at Jackson's congregation in California weren't okay with this occult sensibility, which is ironic because the Witnesses believe that one day, in the Resurrection, billions of dead people—a combination of JWs and worldly people who hadn't gotten a chance to hear the Kingdom message—will stagger out of cemeteries. Organs, sinew, and muscle will re-form in mid-air. What could be more occult than literal zombies? What's the difference between a possessed toy and a reanimated human? A ghost is a ghost is a ghost.

Regardless, the elders threatened to disfellowship Jackson. He wanted to stay in the group, so he begged his team to destroy the *Thriller* tapes, but his legal adviser John Branca refused. Branca convinced Jackson to rationalize creatively, as all JWs must do to reconcile nonsensical rules. He made up a story about actor Bela Lugosi, a staunch Roman Catholic, asking for a disclaimer at the beginning of the film *Dracula* that stated his opposition to vampirism. Couldn't Jackson similarly dance his way out of this? *Thriller* starts with the following title card: *Due to my strong personal convictions, I wish to stress that this film in no way endorses a belief in the occult.*

Jackson went even further in *Awake!*: "I just intended to do a good, fun short film, not to purposely bring to the screen something to scare people or to do anything bad. I want to do what's right. I would never do anything like that again . . . There's all kinds of promotional stuff being proposed on *Thriller*. But I tell them, 'No, no, no. I don't want to do anything on *Thriller*. No more *Thriller*.'"

He obviously didn't honour that promise. When the Jacksons came to Montreal for *The Victory Tour* in 1984, a family acquaintance paid eighty dollars for a pair of tickets, which we all thought was astronomical. He offered to take me, but my mom declined on my behalf, saying that "Michael Jackson wasn't for kids." That may have been true, but now

I think her reluctance had more to do with a strange man proposing an outing with me.

On September 16, 1984, at a time when any other performer would have been rehearsing, Jackson stepped into either my Kingdom Hall in Parc-Extension or the nearby Snowdon Hall. Either way, I wasn't there, but the story trickled down to me. His visit would've been a shock. He would've walked in flanked by bodyguards and taken a seat in the back row. Was anyone tempted to pass Jackson the microphone? What did he think of the hymns, the swelling violins and cymbal crashes, the message that in the coming new world "the former things would pass away"? Could he hear the start of Armageddon in the bass drum? Did it remind him of going to the hall with Tito, Jackie, La Toya, Jermaine, Marlon, Randy, and Janet when they were kids, where they could sing out of pure joy and without pressure or scrutiny?

Jackson made his getaway in a limo before the meeting was over. Geeky teen Witnesses I knew almost killed themselves tailing him through the city, which amounts to committing idolatry—an offence worthy of disfellowshipping. The two nights the Jacksons played Olympic Stadium have since become legendary. Pyrotechnics fried a computer controlling a giant screen and it went dark. The sound in the concrete toilet bowl was terrible, but few people seemed to care. One of those nights, post-concert, Jackson danced on the roof of a van in the middle of the street a few kilometres away. The impromptu crowd confirmed he was indeed bigger than Jehovah.

In 1987, the elders visited Jackson on the set of the video for "Smooth Criminal" to object to its violent content, but he ignored their admonishments. By that point the elders had been threatening to kick him out for years, intimating a choice between his music career and serving Jehovah. He'd already been disciplined—on possibly several occasions—for reasons that likely included sexual suggestiveness in his videos and dance routines. Jackson's breaking point may have been when the elders commanded him to shun his sister La Toya, who hadn't been going to meetings. He disobeyed, and instead disassociated from the Witnesses. The details of Jackson's history with the group remain murky, owing to both the secretive nature of the Watch Tower and the mysteries of his own life. But Jackson's letter of disassociation still feels like one of the Rock & Roll Hall of Fame's most glaring omissions.

I don't remember when I learned of Jackson's disassociation, or if we were ever asked to destroy his records, but it was still a shock to lose our most famous member. What I do remember is the release of the *Bad* album that same year. On the cover, he wears a black leather jacket and stares defiantly at the camera. He looks like one of the worldly people we were warned about. Bad. Those three letters told me all I needed to know about his prospects for living forever.

Yet the Watch Tower's influence continued to permeate Jackson's music. The video for "Heal the World," a song on the 1991 *Dangerous* album, presents a typical Witness narrative: we see sad children, scenes of war and overall unhappiness, until finally, soldiers put down their assault rifles and the children smile again. We hear a message about a possible world without sorrow. The idea of swords being turned into ploughshares is taken directly from Isaiah 2:4, which is repeated endlessly in Society literature as a go-to metaphor for world peace (which, of course, comes after a warmongering God slaughters billions). But Jackson ends up proposing an anti-Jehovah message: Make the world a better place if you care about people. Redemption rests not in divine hands but in human ones, and that happens now, not in the future. I've always loved the song, but now I realize it's for the worst possible reason: musically, it's a replica of what we would sing at the hall, the Kingdom earworms I still can't get out of my head.

———

When Myles, Danny, and I had our band, we looked to music for transcendence instead of to Jehovah. Certain stars were our guides in this work, and Prince was one of them. Growing up, we had understood him to be worldly and someone to avoid. In 1987, the same year Jackson disassociated from the JWs, Prince recorded and produced *The Black Album*, also known as *The Funk Bible*. Using either sped-up or slowed-down vocal tracks, he appeared as different characters on the record, including Camille, his androgynous/feminine alter ego. But he had all five hundred thousand copies of the album destroyed prior to its release, claiming he—or perhaps Camille—was possessed by what he called "Spooky Electric," an entity he seemingly never spoke of again. Somewhere there are thousands of pounds of smashed vinyl in a landfill that never got a proper burial (probably not far from a grave of Smurf limbs). I imagine this seeming rejection of the occult would've pleased some Witnesses if they'd known about it, but I liked Prince for other reasons: his gender nonconformity, his rejection of the music industry's most toxic components, his genius. Who else could write, perform, and produce that way, not to mention play so many instruments?

Unlike Jackson and me, Prince became a Witness long after he'd started making music, joining formally in 2001.

One day in the early aughts, a Minnesota couple opened their door to find him standing there reading scriptures. When the couple objected and said they were Jewish, Prince replied, "Can I finish?" and hung out on their steps for another twenty-five minutes. No one interrupts a performance by Brother Nelson.

As Prince became more devout, he stopped playing some of his racier songs, such as "Darling Nikki." When it had come out on *Purple Rain*—in 1984, before Prince was a Witness—the song's lyrics caused a furor and eventually earned the album one of the first-ever Parental Advisory stickers. Jehovah's Witnesses would've flagged the song for sex, but also for backmasking, a technique that Christian anti-rock crusaders had accused Judas Priest, Led Zeppelin, and other acts of using to conceal subliminal messages. In backmasking, a vocal track appears backward. The record would have to be played in reverse to hear the message intelligibly.

"Normally, of course, people do not play recordings in reverse," said *The Watchtower*. "Yet, when listening to certain musical records, either unscriptural or demonic ideas may be absorbed by a mind left open to improper suggestion." In other words, merely hearing the garbled sounds made you vulnerable to demon attack. The irony is that if the Society had listened to Prince's "Darling Nikki" lyrics backward, it would have discovered a shockingly wholesome message: "Hello, how are you? / Fine, fine 'cause I know that the Lord is coming soon / Coming, coming soon." To me, the song is a perfect example of the kind of cognitive dissonance that grows in the mind of a JW.

In Prince's posthumous memoir *The Beautiful Ones*, collaborator Dan Piepenbring paints Prince's stance on the occult as a consistent one. "When writers ascribed alchemical qualities to his music, they were ignoring the literal meaning of the word, the dark art of turning metal into gold. He would never do something like that. His object was harmony." Yet Prince had no qualms about renting out a Minneapolis theatre so that he could treat members of his crew to a private screening of *Kung Fu Panda 3*, which would be taboo for Witnesses, not only for its martial arts component but also for its undead characters living in the spirit realm. Boiled down, this is a classic case of not practising what one preaches.

Prince addresses this duality directly. "Is he his mother— drinking and swearing and coming on to another human like it's the only chance he'll get?" he asks, referring to himself. "Or is he his father, conducting life as though God were watching every breath—chauvinistic, stubborn, and quick to explode? . . . One minute he's a sweet, quiet little introvert. The next he's either screaming the book of Revelation to someone or he's drunk in the corner of some bar—masturbating."

Yet Prince could still adhere to JW views with frightening precision. He once said this to *The New Yorker* about gay marriage and abortion: "God came to earth and saw people sticking it wherever and doing it with whatever, and he just cleared it all out. He was, like, 'Enough.'" The quote has been disputed, but *The New Yorker* stands by the interview. Even if some context is missing, how could Prince—who many consider to be one of the most sexually liberated artists of all time—veer anywhere *near* thoughts like this?

Easy: cognitive dissonance was hard at work. To be a Jehovah's Witness is to be a living paradox. You must remain *no part of this world* yet interact with everyone in it. You have to exist on the planet while pretending not to breathe its air. You go to work and joke with colleagues as if they won't all be dead soon, bodies littering the street that you'll have to clean up. The rules are nonsensical, and to accommodate them, you must partition your mind at a moment's notice. Over the years, you subdivide it infinitely. You learn to live for loopholes. Somehow, to disbelieve is crazier than to believe. Part of doing this work means a permanent state of living undercover: both hiding your religious zeal in public and pretending at the meetings that you follow the rules perfectly. This is how I could blossom into a little queerdo while distributing magazines that said there was no way I could do both. This is how, at the 2007 Super Bowl, Prince could prowl into "Purple Rain" as actual rain fell, giving an otherworldly performance that would alter the planet's orbit, then on some other day peddle Jehovah door to door as if he were an ordinary minister. Anyone who encounters a Kingdom Song eventually enters this two-state quantum life. It breaks most of us.

———

In my case, leaving the Jehovah's Witnesses didn't exactly translate to ditching an obsession with the occult. When I celebrated my first Halloween at the age of twenty-one, I donned a ghoul mask, knocked on doors in my neighbour-hood without a Watch Tower script for the first time, and begged for candy. Today, I can't shake the feeling that Jackson—a dead man—and I are destined to run into each other one day. I've never gotten over our near miss. It felt like a sign when I came across an article about known ex-JWs that listed MJ first and me last, bookends to a shared story. Sometimes I think, *Maybe once I write and publish this book he'll leave me alone.* I know it sounds delusional.

My ongoing connection to the occult can also manifest in subtler ways. I assumed I was no longer afraid of breakfast foods until I saw the scene in *Muppets from Space* where Gonzo pours milk into his lettered cereal and a memo appears, a message from his family in the distant cosmos. His ping-pong-ball eyes register fear that he immediately transfers to me. It's the same with the scene in *Rosemary's Baby* where rearranged Scrabble tiles reveal that the name of a neighbour is an anagram for a famous occultist. The idea that wooden tiles could be so all-knowing creeps me out. It's bad luck for a writer to be afraid of words this way. All of this makes no sense and embarrasses me.

It seems that Jackson couldn't ditch the occult, either. It's been said that *Ghosts*, his chilling 1996 short film co-written with Stephen King, was the singer's re-embrace of the paranormal after having disavowed *Thriller*. But I think that moment first happened in the final four minutes of the 1991 video for "Black or White" when a panther transforms into Jackson, who dances, screams, and smashes things before turning into a panther again. This time there would be no *mea culpa* for the spiritism behind that kind of transformation.

I don't know if my fear of the paranormal, or my apparent attraction to it, will ever subside. Once a predisposition for the occult takes root in an artist's thinking—either through indoctrination, taking a stand against it, or both—it could become a permanent part of their creative aesthetic. But I might not always recognize the occult when I encounter it, say, in the work of others. Is it paranormal when Sharon Jones curses her cancer out of the concert hall, or when Nick Cave presses a shined shoe onto a fan's chest until the blues seep in? What about when Grace Jones turns the super blood moon over the Hollywood Bowl into her personal disco ball, or when Stevie Nicks disappears into a swirl of gold dust and wool knits?

The Society, for its part, now warns followers not to be obsessed with demons, as if it hadn't fed that very obsession for decades.

———

What used to feel like closeness to Jackson and Prince has now turned into distance. Prince represented freedom to me for most of my post-cult adult life, both in and out of the band, so I naturally felt unsettled when he joined the JWs, who are so vociferously anti-queer. He died a Witness in good standing, which qualifies him to be resurrected in Paradise. It makes me sad to picture him rising from the grave, becoming flesh and blood again, microphone in hand, ditching his entire luminous catalogue for two-bit hymns.

Jackson died an apostate, so according to the doctrine, he won't be resurrected. In the 2019 documentary *Leaving Neverland*, Wade Robson and James Safechuck, who'd been in Jackson's coterie as boys, separately tell their stories of his horrific abuse. We even see Jackson take a young Safechuck to a jewellery store to buy a ring, a symbol of their twisted bond. My hands shake when the adult Safechuck takes it out of the box and shows it to the camera. It's a memento of Neverland, a place so big you could go all day without running into a witness.

These disclosures have made me rethink Jackson's entire discography. It seems his public persona of caring for kids was just a screen for his crimes, one that made believing his victims more difficult. As Wesley Morris writes in *The New York Times*, "But what if all of that change he so notoriously underwent, all the damage he seemed to wear on his body, all the creatures his videos turned him into (werewolves, zombies, a panther, a skeleton), what if his outward self became some semiconscious manifestation of a monster that lurked within?"

What to do with this information? In "With Michael Jackson, It's Different," Jo Livingstone wonders as well. "To try to cancel him would be to point out a criminal at the very heart of the entertainment industry's belief system, and to remove the laurels of the most significant Black artist of the pop age." I wonder what it means for me as a white writer to set down this account, what complexities I've oversimplified and privileges I've overlooked, and if I've claimed common ground with Black artists where little exists.

What is the Watch Tower Society's role in all this? If, at one time, the Society was afraid that Jackson would tarnish its reputation, now it can do that all on its own. A few days before part two of *Leaving Neverland* first aired, the Superior Court of Quebec authorized a class action lawsuit against the group on behalf of current and former Witnesses who'd been sexually assaulted as minors by a fellow member. The headlines hit too close to home: this is where I'd spent almost half my life, and the news could have monumental effects on people I know and love, including some who've suffered this abuse.

This case is only one of many lawsuits against—and investigations into—the Jehovah's Witnesses for policies that enable child sex abuse. For a congregation to investigate such an offence, it is often required that two witnesses to it come forward. The perpetrator can be a witness if they confess. But if no witnesses other than the victim speak up, nothing happens. The child is not believed. The Society claims that its policies have changed, but journalists the world over are not convinced. In some U.S. states, congregations are subject to mandatory reporting laws. When abuse is suspected, elders are instructed to contact the Watch Tower legal department, which often uses legal loopholes to discourage elders from contacting authorities. The Witnesses are loath to involve law enforcement because of the reproach it will bring upon Jehovah, and because they believe earthly agencies represent Satan, not God, and would therefore prosecute them unfairly.

The Society is no more morally upstanding than the members it expels, and the trauma that results from being a Jehovah's Witness can take many forms. It makes sense that the Witnesses latched onto 1980s Stranger Danger and taught members to be afraid of the unseen—it perpetuated the myth that the threat always comes from outside the God-fearing house, when we know the opposite is true. If my upbringing has taught me anything, it's that to assume that demons can ever live outside of us is a mistake.

A LIBRARY FOR APOSTATES

Shortly after I met my partner Wes, they gave me an old McGill University T-shirt they didn't wear anymore. It's a grey crewneck with a faded red-and-white insignia. When I started wearing it, people would ask me what program I was in and I'd have to tell them the truth: none. I don't have a university degree. Wearing the T-shirt began to feel as fraudulent as wearing a rented cap and gown would be. I didn't belong in either.

I've been to McGill, but not to study. Once, on my way to a class there to speak about my first novel, I walked the halls slowly and tried to feel the history, the accretion of knowledge, the anxiety of forty thousand students doing mid-terms, but I felt nothing. While I talked about my book I could tell that the students, who were deep into their own educations, were wondering how to relate their experience to mine: Where did I go to school? What did I study? How did I get from there to authorship? I worried that the first chance they got they would needle me on my academic path and, in so doing, unravel me completely. Was I even qualified to speak here? I didn't tell them about my lack of credentials because I didn't want them to judge me; as for the ones who *wouldn't* judge me, I didn't want them to follow my example because they should forge their own paths in the world.

My impostor syndrome goes deep. A part of me fears that my writing community will take me less seriously if they find out my highest academic honour is a high school diploma. I fear that the writers I mentor will know more about writing theory than I do. To cope, I fake it. I keep question period to a minimum and avoid all discussion about my own education, even though this evasion doesn't feel good. And I don't dare wear a university T-shirt to class whenever I'm invited to speak.

I was deliberately nudged away from school because of having grown up a Jehovah's Witness; the group believes that pursuing worldly knowledge takes followers off the road to Paradise. In their view, college is a place where students plagiarize, binge drink, fuck, and lose all morals while trading God for philosophy and a good GPA.

Just in case any member is foolish enough to let Satan fill their minds at a university, the group has a backup argument: Why bother getting a degree if the world is about to end? You might as well spend the remaining time preaching your heart out. A 1969 issue of *Awake!* puts it like this: "As a young person, you will never fulfill a career that this system offers. If you are in high school and thinking about a college education, it means at least four, perhaps even six or eight more years to graduate into a specialized career. But where will this system of things be by that time? It will be well on the way toward its finish, if not actually gone!" Six years later the Witnesses' prophecy of the world ending in 1975 failed, and yet another generation of acolytes were robbed of an education. According to one study, only nine percent of JWs have an undergraduate degree.

For the Witnesses, the coming Paradise solves the education problem. "We will *not* need doctors or lawyers after Armageddon, but we *will* need carpenters and plumbers and similar construction trades," says Governing Body member Anthony Morris in a video clip. Jesus was a carpenter, after all. The Witnesses maintain that Bible study is the only book-learning necessary. Become a scholar in the

Gospel and it will save you. But can question-and-answer sessions that involve parroting word-for-word responses from the literature be considered an education? "This type of thought generation crushes the human spirit, eliminates critical thinking and autonomy while simultaneously programming the individual toward control-oriented behavior," writes Carrie S. Ingersoll-Wood in "The Educational Identity Formation of Jehovah's Witnesses." The Watch Tower indeed has a vested interest in keeping its members uneducated: the lack of critical thinking makes them easier to control.

This anti-intellectual stance isn't unique to Jehovah's Witnesses. In *Educated*, a memoir about growing up in a fundamentalist and survivalist Mormon family, Tara Westover writes, "An hour later Dad was no longer grinning. Tyler had not repeated his wish to go to college, but he had not promised to stay silent, either. He was just sitting there, behind that vacant expression, riding it out. 'A man can't make a living out of books and scraps of paper,' Dad said. 'You're going to be the head of a family. How can you support a wife and children with *books*?'"

Until reading this passage, I'd forgotten that the faith my mother and I shared hadn't been the only threat to my taking up an academic life. The problem had also been my stepdad, a functionally illiterate man who disparaged books and reading at every turn. He would often pull me out of a book to help him fix his broken-down jalopies: the Torino whose timing chain whined out of sync, the Cutlass Ciera whose rust holes in the floor gave us an unwanted view of Quebec snow. He'd ask me to pass him vise grips, and when I'd fetch needle-nose pliers by mistake he'd look at me with disgust and fling them across the garage. "God damn it! I said vise grips. If it's not written in a book, you have no idea what to do. All that reading and you're useless around a car." For years I'd hand him the wrong thing and he'd insult me for it. The cars never got fixed, and my shame grew into something bigger than a garage could contain.

I started to hide my reading from my stepdad, but he still constantly complained to my mother about this supposed deficit in real-world experience, this failure of masculinity. Sometimes he hit me, and once he tore my earlobe from my head when he tried to lift me up by it. Another time, I had to go to school wearing my mother's foundation to hide a bruise his slap had left on my cheek. Today I live with the persistent feeling that he's right behind me, about to smack my head. I prefer to sit with my back to the wall. And I won't say anything if someone mistakes a Phillips head for a flat head.

I eventually understood that his rage stemmed from his own upbringing, illiteracy, and dyslexia. I had access to a world he didn't. For a few years he studied books and magazines with brothers at the hall, which also served as a form of literacy practice. From my room I could hear him slowly and painfully sounding out the words. He would get many of them wrong and it frustrated him. I don't think he got the support he needed, and I wouldn't be surprised if his dyslexia was the reason he stopped studying *the truth*. I have the feeling that if my stepdad had been able to read auto repair manuals, I might've been his punching bag less often. This is still no excuse for how he treated me.

Again, it's a scene right out of *Educated*. "When Dad saw me with one of those books, he'd try to get me away from them. Perhaps he was remembering Tyler. Perhaps he thought if he could just distract me for a few years, the danger would pass. So he made up jobs for me to do, whether they needed doing or not." I felt the shock of recognition my first time reading this. Had my stepdad actually needed me to pass him tools that were a foot away from him? Had he really needed me to walk to Canadian Tire in the snow for two hours, my toes freezing in thin rubber boots as I trudged along the highway shoulder only to inevitably get him the wrong radiator hose, or was he simply trying to get me away from books?

Given that I had an illiterate, book-shaming stepfather and a mom wrapped up in an anti-education cult, it's either a miracle I turned out to be a writer or a foregone conclusion. I can't tell which teleology I like better. In one narrative, I buck the odds and intervene in my own fate; in the other, I'm hewn of obstacle, of the very matter in my way. And which of the JW arguments did I fall for: that school is a moral cesspool, or that there's no point because of the short time left? The answer to that might be complicated, and probably depends on how hungry I was for the moral cesspools I was supposed to avoid and how firmly I believed the end was near.

If I see my lack of education as primarily the fault of others, I risk losing more agency to a cult bent on taking it all and to an abusive stepdad. If I absorb the blame, I give a pass to people who need to be held accountable. Perhaps binary thinking is the problem. Ultimately, it's not okay for bad things to happen, no matter the result. Maybe the point is that I found role models other than my parents to aspire to.

———

Whenever someone told me I was in a cult it would stick in my mind, even though I never fully believed it. Jehovah's Witness rules didn't feel like restrictions to me—they were the kind of protections a family offered. We took care of one another, and I felt love from all sides. I felt safe in a group that valued peace in a world of violence. I was taught to be compassionate toward strangers, to ask what was going on in their lives, and to offer help. It's ironic that the JWs claim to be removed from society yet spend the most time of anyone meeting their neighbours.

It's okay to remember the good parts about those years, a few people have told me. That might be true, but I don't know if those same people are prepared for me to admit *how many* good parts there were. In her essay "Thin Places," Jordan Kisner says that only when ex-believers find themselves in church, "with the faith atomized in the air," can they truly remember how it was. "Call it late-breaking phantom limb syndrome of the soul." But I haven't been back since I left, so the key to my remembering must lie elsewhere.

What can be called a *cult* is controversial. Is there a single, charismatic leader? What about an advanced indoctrination process? In her essay "What Makes a Cult a Cult?," Zoë Heller writes that "if we accept that cult members have some degree of volition, the job of distinguishing cults from other belief-based organizations becomes a good deal more difficult . . . Acknowledging that joining a cult requires an element of voluntary self-surrender also obliges us to consider whether the very relinquishment of control isn't a significant part of the appeal." This echoes what Amanda Montell says in *Cultish* about how humans "are not helpless drones whose decision-making skills are so fragile that they can be wiped clean at any time ... Simply put, you cannot force someone to believe something they absolutely do not on any level want to believe by using some sort of evil techniques to 'wash' their brain." At the same time, this analysis could turn into victim blaming if taken too far.

Montell prefers the word *cultish* over *cult*, arguing that the latter is an oversimplification, a thought-terminating cliché that obscures, in the listener's mind, the behaviour the speaker is trying to call attention to: what may start as love bombing and end up as isolation. Cognitive dissonance, or what Amber Scorah, author of *Leaving the Witness*, terms "mental contortionism to reconcile the irreconcilable," is another sign of a cultish group. The Witnesses could've done themselves a favour by putting a little more distance between the realities they're trying to keep apart; most hope to live forever in a Paradise earth, which is a change from earlier iterations of the doctrine that said all Witnesses would go to heaven, a place far enough away for vast cognitive leaps not to be so necessary.

In the end, I believe the question of whether the Jehovah's Witnesses are a cult comes down to their stance on education. Any group that claims awareness gained outside of it is flawed or incomplete must have something, or many things, to fear and to hide.

———

Recently, Wes was giving a sex-ed workshop at my former high school, and when they went to look for my grad photo on the wall, there was none to find—not even an empty space, as I had imagined there might be. I'd skipped the photo session that day, the culmination of a year in which I'd let my grades slide. It was as if I'd wanted to disappear. What was the point in trying if I wasn't going to university?

Several of my teachers also seemed not to care. High school guidance counsellors met with me once about continuing education and never followed up. Advisers should be trained to detect when a student's lukewarm attitude to school and lack of career dreams or aspirations might be connected to the anti-intellectual stance of a high-control group. This would put them in a better position to determine whether the severity merits intervention.

I barely graduated. On the last day of class, students gathered around a metal garbage can to burn textbooks. How could I justify spending seventeen dollars on a grad photo to commemorate all this?

One of the many jobs I held after high school was at the family moving company, where I worked for a few years alongside current and former Jehovah's Witnesses. Because JWs are pressured to limit their schooling to community college and vocational training, they rely on trades to pay the bills. Trades are okay because they focus on physical things; the intangible is the domain of the Almighty. Also, as a small contractor, you can work independently and have greater control over who your colleagues are. You can hire other Witnesses. People let us into their homes because we were movers, but they trusted us specifically because Witnesses are known for their honesty, and we were proud of that. And sometimes it's simply handy: because of financial instability, my mom, my stepdad, and I moved from apartment to apartment nearly every year, usually without much warning or planning. The trucks were always available and we were our own best customers.

I pushed dollies, mastered the straps, and learned how to rip tape with my fingertips. We moved pianos down icy stairs and up slippery ramps. We schlepped crystal cabinets across time zones and arranged set pieces for lives we would never live. We moved furniture as if it mattered, as if it wouldn't be destroyed at Armageddon along with the unbelievers who owned it. It was tempting to preach to them—a moving van can be a perfect Trojan horse—but we usually held back. I continued working as a mover even after I left the Jehovah's Witnesses.

As any mover knows, books are the heaviest, so customers often left them for us to pack. And since it turned out that I was good at boxing them, I'd often find myself on book duty. Electricity shivered through me as I plucked books off shelves and wrapped them in newsprint. I categorized entire worlds of knowledge closed to a JW, the kind of texts I would have otherwise read at university. On one job, I was ushered through a false wall panel into a secret library of Masonic tomes, spines bearing the telltale Square and Compasses and the All-Seeing Eye. Like the JWs, the Freemasons produced their own literature, but they permitted a wider reading latitude than we did. I stole hours off the clock to read, then sealed the boxes and emerged through the hidden door for pizza and sunlight. I still wonder why that family felt the need to hide their books.

In her memoir *The Truth Book*, Joy Castro writes about the taboo of reading non–Watch Tower material, and how she used to smuggle library books onto the school bus by hiding them in the lining of her coat. She remembers a book that "features a girl who goes to college, something Witnesses do not do, something no one in our family has done. College, as forbidden as sex . . . I've begun to plot a private future." I'm intrigued by this articulation of escape. Every apostate must build their own library of contraband texts to slip into their coat. In many cases the texts will not exist, and the apostate will have to write them.

Eventually, my curiosity about school grew too big to ignore. In 1997, when I was twenty-one—three years after I'd left my faith and become an apostate—I applied as a mature student to the Fine Arts program at Concordia University and got in. The admissions panel were intrigued by my shabby portfolio; I showed them blurry black-and-white photos in a three-ring binder and a childish painting I'd done on a shoebox. Perhaps they saw past my lack of an artistic practice and recognized my desire to learn, my thirst for knowledge, my largely unused creative capacities that needed a place to flourish. My many privileges—white, cis, able, English-speaking, male, citizen—helped. I circled classes in the program booklet, not fully realizing what I was getting myself into.

At first, things went well. I developed a deeper grasp of the world outside a biblical eschatology. I learned that Susan

Sontag and Roland Barthes were gods, vapours who could float through my mind and change how images ordered the universe for me. Black-and-white photography was somehow less monochromatic than the blood-soaked sketches of Armageddon I had grown up with. The simple shapes of Paradise landscapes faded away to make room for a more complex visual language. Morality gave way to theory.

I was excited by this new opening for a while, until I slid into the same apathy I'd felt in high school. I mangled quotes and turned in barely legible essays, if I turned them in at all. I was more interested in getting high on darkroom chemicals than in completing my photography assignments. And yes, I was getting high on other substances, too, though I'm not sure the Watch Tower had been right about the corrupting nature of college. My fellow students all seemed to take their studies seriously. If anything, I was a bad influence on them. I became the bane of my interdisciplinary arts professor when I brought a fan club of friends to her tiny class of ten students. We sat on tables and snapped bubble gum. The professor soon asked me to leave and not come back. She didn't think I was student material. I was defiant and wanted to prove that getting a degree isn't the only valid life path. At the time, I didn't see the irony in the anti-intellectual stance I'd taken.

I stopped going to all my classes. I never even formally dropped out, unaware of the impact it would have on my GPA. I lasted only a semester and a half at Concordia, partly because I wanted to abdicate responsibility for a while in exchange for an adolescence that religion had stolen from me, but also because I wanted to go out and grab the post-education life that school had taught me to envision. I still felt doubt and guilt, however, about blowing my chance at school, when so many people who don't have my privileges never get that chance to begin with.

A year later, on a trip to a used bookstore, I discovered Mark Dery's 1999 book *The Pyrotechnic Insanitarium: American Culture on the Brink*. Dery explores millennial angst by writing around the edges of the human condition: our death drive, our obsession with the gruesome. I fell from the precipice of every page. It was the kind of grimoire that as a Witness I wouldn't have been allowed to touch. Reading it, I felt the same thrill I did when I packed books as a mover. It's odd that this non-JW text taught me more about doomsday than I'd ever learned to date.

In one chapter, Dery writes about how "evil clowns" propose an imperviousness that is "perfectly adapted to life in a hall of media mirrors where reality and its fun house double are increasingly indistinguishable." In other words, a clown's forced greasepaint smile might be the ideal response to attacks on reality, and to the information and sensory overload that Dery calls "info-vertigo." It dawned on me that I was this clown. This smile was one I'd practised and mastered when I was a preacher, when everything in the world was an attack on my religious reality. Later, when partaking of the "info-vertigo" I needed to free myself, I kept this smile as protective armour, because attacks on reality—including the new one I was forging—had by then become a normal feature of daily life. Connecting with Dery's book was proof that even outside school, I'd need literature to make sense of the world.

Clowns would remain a theme of my enlightenment. Years later, I would see "Little Fear of Lightning," an episode of HBO's Emmy-winning series *Watchmen*, about a group of Jehovah's Witness youth who go to a carnival on a preaching mission. (It's not something we would ever do, but I appreciate the imagery.) The young men disembark onto the grounds of a carnival and step into a frenzy of late-summer lust. One of the men, Wade, walks through a tableau of *Watchtower*-style cautionary tales: teens French kissing before marriage, freaking out to devil music, thrashing around in leather duds. It's a playground for heathens. He preaches to a woman who seduces him in a funhouse only to steal his clothes. Wade sees his nakedness refracted in the mirrors, then an explosion knocks him to the floor. He eventually regains consciousness and stumbles outside to find the park littered with bodies. The woman who stole his clothes is dead in a pool of her own blood, her face frozen in horror. The Ferris wheel carries the dead. This is exactly what Armageddon is supposed to look like—what else could it be?—but it still shocks him into a scream. *What happened? What happened?* We zoom out over the carnage and across the Hudson River, past a flaming and collapsed Madison Square Garden, then past a giant squid clinging to several midtown Manhattan buildings.

Somehow, seeing all this still doesn't answer Wade's question.

———

I cringe at the words *self-taught* and *autodidact* for their arrogance, for how solitary they make the process of learning sound, which is the opposite of my experience. If growing up a JW had created a vacuum in my mind, I later filled the vacuum with books, which ended up filling it with people. I met archetypes that were new to me, both on the page and in real life. I wrote to authors whose achievements occurred both inside and outside of academia; many of them became my mentors and then my friends.

I haven't needed school to know what to read. My partner Mark and I have taken up residence in the great used bookstores of the world, where we hunt rare first editions, waiting patiently for them to show their deckled edges. I get book recommendations from a multitude of sources and I assign myself homework every day. When my friend Ricky gave me a copy of Bohumil Hrabal's novel *Too Loud a Solitude*, I recognized myself in the narrator, a paper crusher who rescues books and who fears getting killed in his sleep by the shelves that sag over his bed. That's probably how I'm going to go, too.

When someone tells me I don't need a degree, they're totally right: I've managed to get published without one, so I'm living proof that school isn't the only path to building a writing career. When applying for opportunities, my writing experience is often accepted as an equivalent to a degree. Still, when I hear the message that I don't need one, my brain computes that I shouldn't try to reach higher, self-improve, or grow in ways I think might be good for me. A part of me hears echoes of Jehovah's Witnesses.

So in 2020 I decided to go back to school. I applied for readmission to Concordia, got in, and started the process of bumping up my 0.2 GPA. I got an A in my first class. I'm the oldest one there and I do my homework with pride and terror. When I was younger and certain of everything, I absorbed very little. Now that I'm certain of nothing, I finally have the chance to shift the foundations of what I know. My heart is a bibliography. I belong wherever books take flight. Paradise, unlike what I was taught growing up, is a classroom of my own making, a place where I can be both professor and student if I wanted to. In Paradise, I will not be afraid of question period. I will wear any T-shirt I want.

And in case this is the end, this is exactly how I want to spend it.

SINNING IN A SECOND LANGUAGE

In 2004 I was twenty-eight and living in Montreal, working at my family's moving company in a job that felt like as much of a dead end as the relationship I was in. I needed a fresh start, as far away from my then life as possible.

Because I hadn't finished my undergrad, opportunities for me to work abroad were limited. I'd heard about teaching English as a second language—how it was a thing that young, lost North Americans did—and thought, *I could do that.* I was young. I was lost. I took ESL night classes for three months and got my teaching certificate. On DavesESLcafe.com, I discovered private language schools where I could teach ESL without a university degree. I had several exchanges with Program-Bell in Poznań, Poland, and I could feel we were a fit.

I also sensed that Poland's renaissance aligned with my own—2004 was the year the country joined the European Union. Its public image was one of promise and opportunity. There was the hope that Poland might be able to ditch its Eastern Bloc drabs for the haute couture of the West, its lingering Soviet austerity for the bounties of Berlin, Paris, and London. This was a new dawn, and everyone was going to know about it. Now that Europe's doors were "open" to Poles, they could presumably travel and work in dozens of countries they couldn't before. Stocks in speaking English—a global and colonial currency I held—went up, and suddenly parents were sending their kids to class in droves. Business was good for Program-Bell. I signed an employment contract and told my partner, which sealed our breakup. One of my final jobs as a mover was the sad task of divvying up our things into separate boxes, most of which went into storage. I got a work visa, bought a one-way ticket, and packed my bags.

Once I got to Poznań, the owners of Program-Bell made sure I fell in love not just with the school, but also with the city. Poznań sits on the border with Germany and sees itself as a gateway to Western Europe; it's modern, functional, and a good place to do business, yet still ancient in a charming way. One of the main tourist attractions is the clock tower in the town plaza where two goats come out at noon to butt heads. To me, one goat represents tradition and the other a relentless hunger for futurity. Together they spark a tension that shapes the country. I suppose it made sense, then, that Program-Bell saw itself as a finishing school for diplomats.

The school oversaw my accommodations and gave me a spacious, sunlit place in a building on Ulica Strzałkowskiego, from which I could walk to school every day. When I told people my street, they would pause a moment, then ask if I'd been to the McDonald's on the corner—as if that were the only place where someone from North America would want to eat.

My building's most curious feature was the security guard who sat in a tiny cubicle on the ground floor near the front door, with a window facing the street. He'd sip instant coffee, read the newspaper, and make small talk. He was very old and often slept in his chair but would rouse himself and mumble greetings when I came home, pretending he'd been awake the whole time.

I should clarify that I didn't speak Polish, and that the school liked it that way. It was in their best interest for me *not* to learn the language. They marketed me as a "native speaker": someone students couldn't speak Polish with if English got too difficult for them. I had a phrasebook and studied it assiduously, but I still couldn't exchange more than a few words with the security guard. We had a perfect symbiosis: he pretended my Polish was perfect, and I pretended he was always awake.

My language troubles followed me everywhere. Near my place, there was a cafeteria where I had lunch several times a week, a glorious Cold War holdover with hearty soups, fruit crêpes, and enough pierogis to populate heaven with. I would often order the wrong thing and have to suffer through one surprise delicacy after another, which, I now realize, was no incentive to learning the language at all. When I tried to order *zapiekanka*—a type of fast food that resembles half a baguette covered in mayo, ketchup, and melted cheese—I sometimes mistakenly asked for Zakopane, a resort town in the Tatra Mountains in the south of the country. My trouble buying condoms at the pharmacy, however, wasn't an issue of grammar, vocabulary, or pronunciation. A colleague, a native Pole, told me it was a *moral* incomprehension of why I would need them.

My first project with the school was running three two-week summer camps back to back. I and my new friends Aaron and Becky were counsellors in charge of up to thirty-five kids in a historic castle in the woods. Our job was to keep them alive just long enough to learn the future conditional. We ran point around the clock: bee stings, teen romances gone wrong, first periods, random nausea, and the million other ways a summer evening could unfold unexpectedly. Some of the older kids switched rooms in the middle of the night by hopping window ledges from turret to turret, risking a ten-metre drop (alas, there was no moat). We suspected weed but didn't find any. We ran ragged with tasks, but it was all worth it—and it was murder to say goodbye at the end of each two-week stint.

Once back at the school in the city, Aaron, Becky, and I continued to stick together. We hung out in the library, where we worked on our lesson plans, cued cassette tapes to play in class for listening comprehension tests, and traded disciplinary tips. We formed an alliance of sorts. Becky was from Ontario and Aaron from Illinois. We three stood out from the Brits at the school, not only in accent but also in teaching style. We nurtured our cachet through a raft of inside jokes.

The adults in class were serious, and so were most of the teens, which surprised me. I had assumed that many of them attended language class merely to up their pan-European earning power and placate their parents, but the students had their own motivations. Learning a new language—including falling into its inevitable traps and black holes—rewires the brain, as I would later learn. Language is at the core of our identities. It can be both thought-expanding and thought-terminating, depending on who is deploying the language and why. The students could sense all this and knew its power. Sure, we observed apathy in them, but we also watched new love, friendships, and ideas blossom in a second language. We saw political minds awaken using words the students had been searching for their whole young lives.

If ESL makes world-expanding possible, it's not because it gives insight into the language. English grammar books are written with a kind of snooty seriousness, with little self-awareness and no acknowledgment of how the language is a sham, a patchwork of exceptions. What no one talks about is that English teachers around the world owe their jobs to these exceptions. If a student asks why something is funny, watch the prof squirm for a bit before retreating smugly inside a tower of insider knowledge. *Humour is one of the most difficult things to learn in a new language. Study for a few more years and you might be able to laugh with us.* This is the power of imperialism and colonialism: the power to mandate and teach a language whose rules are unknowable to most, even to those who teach it. Now imagine ESL teachers *grading* any of this and you've got a farce on your hands, but one that everyone's happy to go along with.

———

What I hadn't expected in my year in Poland was the social pressure to attend church. Sonja, a friend of the school, took me in on Christian holidays, partly to make sure I didn't feel left out, and partly to make sure I appreciated how fabulously Poland did holidays. On the Day of the Dead she and her husband and sons brought me to a cemetery, where we walked through the maze of tombstones lit up by thousands of windproof candles in coloured glass pots. *This is one way to wake the dead*, I thought. In the Witness version of resurrection, bodies simply break through the hard ground and re-form under whatever clothes they were buried in, which is far less beautiful than souls released in explosions of colour.

Although I'd started to celebrate Christmas a few years earlier with my ex, that year in Poland I was planning to spend it alone. Sonja was horrified by the idea and insisted I come to her house for a few days. We feasted on carp they'd kept alive in the bathtub until slaughter—a beloved Polish tradition—and we went to midnight mass at a half-dozen churches packed to the doors. The city was soaked in song. We passed nativity scenes on nearly every corner.

It was never Sonja's intention to convert me. She could see the godlessness in my eyes when I ritually cracked hard-boiled eggs with her sons at Easter, but it didn't bother her. She understood that there was room in these rituals for everyone—an excuse for togetherness, a chance to address our humanity. I started to see what she meant, yet I never felt safe enough to reveal my queerness, which, if I'd been paying attention, told me all I needed to know about this second brush with religion. How could I feel safe when queerphobic protesters, egged on by the Church, outnumbered Pride marchers across the country and pelted them with bricks and bags of shit?

That didn't stop me from visiting St. Mary's Basilica, a Gothic construction and one of the largest brick churches in the world, while on a trip to Gdańsk. Traces of fires, lootings, and bombings mark it forever. The nave is a white upside-down sky whose shadow play tells the story of centuries. I was in the heart of evil Christendom, one of the first "false" religions that will be abolished at Armageddon, according to *The Watchtower*. Catholicism has always been a favourite target of the Witnesses. "Her religion is the fruit of the great apostasy from true Christianity...The clergy of Christendom claim to be in God's temple and have represented themselves as teachers of Christianity. But their doctrines are far removed from Bible truth, and they continually bring God's name into disrepute." In nearly every illustration of Armageddon in Watch Tower publications, a heavenly fist comes crashing down on a cathedral and its rooftop crucifix.

All this was at odds with the peace I felt sitting in that empty basilica first thing in the morning. So after that I set out in search of more churches, which isn't difficult to do in a country that's ninety-eight percent Catholic. I took the train to Kraków and fell in love with churches that had escaped bombing, as if the spires were too wispy to be noticed by German pilots. I sat in the back of the Franciscan Church, not entirely sure what I was doing there. But I knew I liked the way the darkness held me. It was difficult to see the frescoes because they were obscured by the soot of old fires. The char was a reminder to pray and hold close all that's dear before it vanishes.

Also in Kraków, I stumbled into a St. Mary's—yes, another one—and was surprised to see how different it was from the one in Gdańsk. Here, the vault was a deep indigo scattered with luminescent stars. I got lost in its nighttime aesthetic until I couldn't ignore the altar any longer, the wood frames that shot high into the air, the gold gilt and lacquer as forbidding as it was beautiful. When something takes decades to make, you're supposed to feel in awe of it. You're not supposed to think about what inconsistencies might have crept in as different generations of craftspeople died and took over from one another. I wasn't supposed to notice that some church bricks didn't match.

But my true induction into Catholicism was at school. Every Wednesday I had to take a commuter train a hundred kilometres southeast to teach three classes. The town of Ostrów Wielkopolski, while tiny, distant, and somewhat dreary, was no punishment to me. I grew to enjoy these sojourns into the countryside, where I figured I could commune with the *real* Poland: coal burning, radish farming, hyper religious, and—strangely—deep into heavy metal. I got to try out some of the Polish I was teaching myself, and it was improving. Every week I told the owner of a local eatery that he had the best chicken in all of Poland—as if I'd tasted all of it—and if he didn't accept the compliment, then at least he understood it.

My first class of the day was with the local Roman Catholic priest who lived in the manse next door to the church. Alfred was a lover of languages and seemed to be competing with Pope John Paul II for how many he could speak. He could never remember whether I was there to teach him English or German. I brushed up on my Vatican-speak and designed lesson plans around church vocabulary. He found tenses a nightmare, but as a jokester, he could always land a punchline. I wonder how many ESL teachers he'd burned through before he became my charge. *Have you taught this man?* I felt like posting online, along with a picture of him smiling in front of a massive library of ancient texts and travel magazines, his finger pointing out a destination on a spinning globe. Alfred always sent me home with something, a gift to remember him by until the following Wednesday, as if I could possibly forget him. At Easter he gave me a three-foot chocolate bunny, which I had to take with me on the train back to Poznań—my seatmate.

There were many things I didn't know about Alfred until recently. He was an author and local historian, with several published books about wooden churches in the Wielkopolski region. In 2019, when he was living in the House of John Paul II, a retirement home for priests, the Polish government honoured him as a hero for his role in the Solidarity movement: in 1981 he'd been prison chaplain of a local detention centre for union activists held under martial law, where he organized activities for hunger strikers. It makes me sad that throughout the time we spent together, he never spoke about this. But I also never revealed myself to Alfred. I wasn't out to many people in Poland, and Ostrów Wielkopolski happened to be in a deep part of my closet.

After my class with Alfred, but before going back to Poznań every week, I had to teach two classes at the

Program-Bell outpost in town. The first hour I taught kids and the second hour adults, including Greta, a former nun. I didn't find it strange when she gave me homemade pie or soup after class, or a little stuffed teddy bear holding a heart. Part of me thought these gestures were Polish customs I simply hadn't been exposed to yet. I thought about the innocence of the chocolate bunny that Alfred had given me. Also, I was new to teaching, and hadn't yet developed a good set of boundaries to guide me in teacher-student relationships. And I was so awash in excitement about being in Poland that I didn't put up many defences, period.

So I wasn't overly alarmed when Greta gave me a train schedule she'd transcribed by hand, in case I wanted to come and visit her on my days off. I started to clue in that something was wrong the day she turned in a written assignment about a dream she'd had: a nun in soft pyjamas awakens to find an English teacher in her room. That was it. I informed the school, but it was already too late. In my naïveté I'd given Greta my cell number, which she started to call incessantly— once, seventeen times in a row—even though I never picked up. I had to change the number. The Program-Bell owners chastised me for letting things get that far, then kicked Greta out of the school. She came back once and scuffled with the receptionist outside my classroom door to try to see me again. She apparently sent me love letters for months, care of the school, which my bosses promptly destroyed.

If this was God calling me back to religion, He sure had a strange way of doing it.

———

I find it no accident that the next year, a few months before I left Poland, I started to write a novella about Jehovah's Witness punks in Florida who rebel against their faith. I didn't own a computer, so I wrote on lunch breaks and after hours on the communal desktop in the school cafeteria, fuelling my drafts with instant coffee. When colleagues asked what I was working on I wouldn't tell them, and I was reluctant to cede the computer when they needed to check email or print class handouts. I didn't plan the writing; the text just started coming out of me, an entity all its own. I visited Aaron when he was staying in Kraków and locked myself in his apartment to write longhand in notebooks for days until my novella draft was finished. I paused only to buy beer and kielbasa from a nearby market. Later, I borrowed Aaron's laptop to type out what I hadn't already typed at the cafeteria.

Tomek, a teacher colleague, grilled me regularly about what I was writing. I finally told him, and he said, "Wow, you have so much anger about this." That confused me. It had never occurred to me that I'd been carrying anger around, least of all over religion. Tomek was right, of course. On paper, I had many things to be angry about: that my mother would rather have died than accept a blood transfusion, leaving me motherless; that I'd been actively discouraged from getting an education, putting me years behind my peers in developing critical thinking skills; that I'd given years of free labour to a group all too happy to financially exploit its members; that my sexuality had made me deserving of death; that my sister, Catrina, had been—and continued to be—exposed to a group that hates women.

I'm still angry, of course. I'm angry that although I speak to my mother every week and we know how to show each other love in many ways, we are, and probably always will be, intellectually estranged from each other. I'm angry when people tell me I should be thankful she doesn't shun me. If the weather is the most profound thing she and I can talk about, haven't I already lost her?

I'm angry that the people I love have to contend with this sick past I come from, and with its fallout. I'm angry that I'm guilty of indoctrinating people and have no way to apologize to them. I'm angry that my nonbinary partner Wes isn't recognized as a human being by religious fundamentalist types, and that these same people brand my polyamorous relationship model a deviance. I'm even angry about not being able to access anger easily. My partners, friends, and sister continually remind me of the need to stick up for myself, to maintain my dignity, to acknowledge that I have the right to seek justice, apologies, and healing, but it's still difficult. When I do, I'm sometimes told that it seems as though I'm *trying* to be angry.

Paul Lisicky writes about this elusiveness in his memoir *Later: My Life at the End of the World.* "Am I angry? It doesn't occur to me that I might be one of those people who turn their anger inward, against themselves, to make it look like another emotion—inertia or loneliness so I don't have to think of myself as an angry person. But why am I opposed to the anger in myself? Why can't I make a home in it? Is it just that anger lives in absolutes, slams the door on nuance? Is it only that anger doesn't always feel so good, like running six miles without any of the endorphins?"

Up until that time in Poland, I'd done everything to prevent myself from acknowledging my anger and its rightful place in my life—and Tomek could feel it in me. I'd made my novella characters so different from myself that I had difficulty relating to anything in their struggles around leaving the Jehovah's Witnesses. I sabotaged any chance for the story to be therapeutic. When it came out a year later with a Canadian micropublisher, all anyone wanted to know was about my personal experiences, and I'd shoot back defensively, "But what about these fucked-up Floridians I wrote about?" It's a lesson that didn't stick. Four years after that I wrote a novel about queerphobia in Poland, perhaps a chance to expiate my guilt over remaining closeted in a country that hated me so much. The book was bursting with religion yet gave me little pause to think about my own religious experiences growing up. Strike two.

Regardless, that year of writing was the start of a new world for me: that of addressing my cult upbringing, if indirectly. This reckoning shouldn't have come as a surprise. After all, I had just left my partner and my hometown and airdropped myself into an environment that was completely new to me, confronted by a language I could barely speak. After leaving the Jehovah's Witnesses I never thought I'd be so intimately wrapped up in the manuscripts and rituals of another religion, but there I was, lighting votive candles and teaching clergy how to do their jobs in my language. Circumstances were set up for my code to be disrupted, for a shift just seismic enough to get me thinking about things in a new way. And perhaps most significantly, that was around the time I started to read apostate websites—to finally confront the facts about my upbringing that I knew were available to me. The corruption. The deceit. The hypocrisy. The gaslighting. I had avoided making this contact for years, partly for fear of what I would find, but also because of a feeling I was just becoming aware of: ex-JWs, for all the mutual support they give, can be bad reminders of a past I find myself wishing, on some days, to forget completely. Imagine that: a memoirist who wishes to forget.

In *Leaving the Witness* Amber Scorah writes about moving from British Columbia to China, where preaching was banned, so that she could make friends with strangers in order to secretly convert them, which would mean suggesting that their Chinese culture and beliefs were inferior to her own. "I was an uneducated preacher posing as an English teacher, my presence here not what I claimed it was. I was out to change the course of other people's lives, and their children's lives, and their children's children's lives. I somehow had the effrontery to try to alter the course of their history, to urge these people to make over their lives into the shape of mine, when I had never even considered how my own life had come to look as it did." In these new surroundings, continuing as a Jehovah's Witness no longer made sense to Scorah. She would go on to leave the religion while still in China.

The more I researched, the more links I discovered between ESL, travel, and religious disaffection. In *Interior States*, Meghan O'Gieblyn writes that when she left Moody Bible Institute, she "took a volunteer position with some missionaries in Ecuador, which was merely an elaborate escape plan—a way to get away from Moody and my parents. Three months into the commitment, I moved to a town in the south of the country where I didn't know anyone, got a job teaching ESL, and stopped going to church entirely."

Being immersed in a new language has neurolinguistic effects that, as Amanda Montell argues in *Cultish*, can remake our very minds: "From the crafty redefinition of existing words (and the invention of new ones) to powerful euphemisms, secret codes, renamings, buzzwords, chants and mantras, 'speaking in tongues,' forced silence, even hashtags, language is the key means by which all degrees of cultlike influence occur."

Montell explains the various steps of the grift. First, the would-be cult leader uses language to love bomb, to make the listener feel understood, special. The words set the followers apart and help them recognize one another in the darkness of a world seemingly without guidance or direction. Built into this language of belonging is an us-versus-them dichotomy. There's no middle ground. At the same time, the follower might be confused by the jargon, becoming dependent on the leader for decoding it, which is key for spiritual understanding. The language, once embedded in the convert, shapes a new reality inside them, making them willing to act in ways that would conflict with what their former selves stood for.

"The goal is to make your people feel like they have all the answers, while the rest of the world is not just foolish, but inferior . . . It all inspires a sense of intrigue, so potential recruits will want to know more; then, once they're in, it creates camaraderie, such that they start to look down on people who aren't privy to this exclusive code. The language can also highlight any potential troublemakers, who resist the new terms—a hint that they might not be fully on board with the ideology and should be watched." Reading all this, I realize I'm indeed a creature formed by cultish language, spouting the babel of whatever public or private hell-du-jour I need to survive. I've worked in marketing and have both internalized and deployed the talk. I was born into the Jehovah's Witnesses, which means I never joined the group. Given the chance to hear their message for the first time, would I be susceptible to it? Probably so—just another thing for me to be angry about.

It only makes sense, then, that when one's language system is disrupted a second time—usually by the follower and outside forces in tandem—self-awareness becomes possible again. Many have written about disruption techniques for reversing the effects of the neurolinguistic programming that many cults use. I believe that this disruption is made easier when the follower is immersed in a language other than the one they were indoctrinated in. If this is true, I wonder what learning English made possible for my students, and if there were any recovering former members of a high-control group among them who found freedom in the inanities of phrasal verbs.

I also wonder whether I joined another cultish group when I became an ESL teacher. As newbie evangelists of the English language, getting certified so that we could spread the good news of our mother tongue in lands near and far, weren't we, as Scorah writes, "out to change the course of other people's lives"? The ESL profession is full of jargon repeated endlessly in a feedback loop. It was drilled into our heads that we were never to give the answer to students, nor could we abandon them in this quest completely. We had to *elicit* the answer, to tease it out of them with prompts. "Elicit! Elicit! Elicit!" we'd echo to one another in mutual evaluations. Good grades weren't enough—we wanted to call forth the very souls of our students. Even though I no longer teach English, *elicit* remains for me what Montell calls "loaded language."

Like many companies, private language schools are cliquish to the max: staff members are expected to do everything together or risk social isolation, which might go double for expats. Ever since the day Aaron, Becky, and I met, we formed our own sub-clique. But it's possible what we did together wasn't so much cultlike behaviour as it was resistance to it; maybe we banded together because we knew we didn't belong, that we would always somehow be outsiders.

———

During my last few months in Poland in 2005, Pope John Paul II was sick and deteriorating quickly. The tenor in the country changed as newscasts showed live cams of the room on an upper floor of the Vatican building where his deathbed was rumoured to be. We all watched the dim light behind the curtains for a sign. Instinctively, I bought votive candles, knowing I would eventually need them.

JP II wasn't just the pontiff, he was the Polish pontiff. He was Karol Wojtyła, the handsome young man from a Kraków seminary who skied in Zakopane (not *zapiekanka*) and made funny faces for paparazzi. This was the pope credited with giving the Solidarity movement a boost and helping to bring down the Iron Curtain. The day he died, my school closed for a week, along with the rest of the country. This isn't a euphemism. Stores blacked out their windows, advertisements came down off billboards, and children wore commemorative armbands. Apartment windows and tram cars flew the Vatican colours. It was the single largest outpouring of grief I've ever witnessed. Traffic snarled because mourners made giant crosses out of candles in the middle of intersections and chanted *"Santo subito!"*—canonize him right away. They gathered every night in the park where in 1956 over a hundred thousand people protested Soviet rule. At the time, not everyone made it out alive. One of the dead was thirteen-year-old Roman Strzałkowski, after whom my street was named, the only one in Poland with the honour. I understood that he was the reason people paused when I told them where I lived.

The night the pope died, I lit a candle, walked downstairs to the front door, and gave it to the security guard. It was the only language we needed.

WE ARE THE ONES HELD

When I was eighteen going on nineteen, I took a three-month bartending course at a private school. We were a class of thirty hopefuls. The instructor gave us weeks of arcane theory about different types of gin, which we read as nostalgia for a time when his life was wild and full, unlike now, lecturing to flunkies who couldn't remember how many olives a martini took. Eventually, we got to make and taste our own concoctions. I couldn't admit that my Long Island Iced Tea was a failure; I simply told myself its layers were as complex and inscrutable as my own. Not once did the instructor ask if any of us were driving home. The school disappeared the week after I graduated and a photocopy shop took its place.

I threw on a suit and handed out resumés to three hundred bars in downtown Montreal. I had no concept that correcting typos with Wite-Out was unprofessional. Bar management either laughed me out or never got in touch with me. They didn't think I understood alcohol well enough to tend to scotch hounds three times my age, which I took as an insult. The ultimate litmus test was when I applied to a restaurant where the owner said I could have the job if I could make him a gimlet. As it happened, that was one of the few drinks I *hadn't* practised. My Tom Collins, grasshopper, and whisky sour were impeccable, but it hardly mattered. "It's a gimlet, not an omelette," he told me when I asked whether it had egg white. I failed because it was an old man's drink: rarefied and completely off my radar. Now I know it's two parts gin, one part Rose's Lime Cordial. In the absence of cordial, you can use lime juice and simple syrup. Add a splash of soda and you get an older version of the cocktail. But who's grading me now?

———

When you *hold your liquor*, you are the flask, the tumbler, the highball. Drink sloshes around and nothing leaks out. You hide the effects of a buzz like a pro, but the rest is vague.

Technically, how much can you hold? Can you hold anything else? Does being waterproof also mean nothing can get *in*?

———

"Remember me?" said the random text message. I did, but only vaguely, so I asked him to send clues: events, places, mutual friends. Any details I could latch onto. He sent pics, which brought it all flooding back. The operas he sang in a ruby rhinestone shirt. Our dripping hot sex. The time we walked downtown in the snow, lay on our backs inside the giant Christmas tree at Place du Canada, and gazed up into the blinking lights. He came to some of my classes and parties, and we went to activist meetups together. It's not a stretch to say we were boyfriends. That was twenty-three years ago. Some memory fade is understandable, but a complete blackout? It had to be the alcohol. Great. I'm a memoirist whose memories have bottle-shaped holes in them.

———

At some point, the cocktails and shots swirl as a singular mix-ture, the same indistinguishable mud. The way to remember a drink is to name it. Jägermeister and milk over ice is called a *Milk Jagger*.

———

I met my first boyfriend, Jeff, when I was twenty-one, right after I was first accepted at Concordia. I fell for him completely. I took hundreds of photos of him on romantic picnics so that I could moon over his smirk, his chin scruff, his faraway dreaminess on weeks he was too busy to see me. I wrote him effusive love letters and mailed them the few blocks to his apartment. One night when I was shaving before one of our dates, I dragged the razor the wrong way down my neck and opened dozens of little cuts. I apologized to him for showing up dotted with bloody Kleenex bits, but he just laughed it off. At the time, I'm not sure I realized why I was so afraid of losing him. My desperation must've had a stink to it.

Another night we were at a lounge, sunken into its red velvet sofas—Jeff, me, a few of my friends, and the resident bedbugs. We listened to 90s trip-hop and fell into a time warp. I was tippling heavily on vodka cranberry. If I were looking for an excuse, I'd say I was in despair over the feeling that Jeff was going to leave me. In that state, I was oblivious to the nature of self-fulfilling prophecies, how we conjure what we fear through the fear itself. Perhaps we do this subconsciously to speed up our fates, to bring about the end we think we deserve, to prove our low self-esteem and negative self-opinions right. Add substances and voilà: a perfect downward spiral. But perhaps by that point I'd had my fill of interpreting prophecy.

I started to feel sick. I ran to the bathroom and puked buckets of red bile onto the floor around the toilet. My knees stuck to the cranberry flypaper of my own humiliation. I could hear the Chemical Brothers through the bathroom door, and it made me sicker. I heaved for ten minutes until Jeff came and held my strawberry-blond bangs out of the bowl, even though I didn't want him to see me like that. The homophobic security guard almost busted the door down, but he needn't have worried—Jeff and I had long since stopped having sex. Back on the sofa, I fell on him with one of my Marlboro Lights and burned a cherry into his hand. He yelped. I don't remember if that happened before or after I puked; whether he cradled my head with a punctured palm, the hole still hot with my stupidity, or whether I branded him as a thank-you for his help.

Jeff left me after about eight months. I was indignant. I didn't feel I deserved to be broken up with. I called him to complain, and when I heard a voice in the background, I accused him of cheating on me. In my rage, I couldn't imagine that voice simply being a friend's—as if it was any of my business. I don't believe we'd ever even discussed monogamy. Acting the jealous lover wasn't authentic to who I am—my heart is a polyamorous beehive. What was I trying to accomplish with my childish performance? Whatever the case, I did my best to avoid confronting the truth: that drinking had contributed to the end of our relationship. An empty bottle is full of wonder.

Twenty years later, Mark and I were chilling in the lobby of a theatre in Toronto during the intermission of a performance piece when Jeff floated into my sightline. Time melted. I said hi. He looked at me for a moment, smiled politely, and walked away. Snubbed again—I couldn't believe it. Shaking, I took my seat, but moments before the second act started, Jeff came bounding down the aisle to where we were sitting. "Oh, it's *you*! Let's talk after the show!" I guess I wasn't the only one who could forget a boyfriend's face. Our catch-up was fun but ridiculously insufficient. Even though I didn't see any cigarette-burn scars on his hands, I still had plenty to apologize to him for.

———

Brio and rum with an orange twist is called a *Brionardo DiCaprio*. The *Milk Jagger* now goes for twelve dollars in a part of town I can no longer afford.

———

I used to free pour through every writing session until I reached a level of drunkenness I thought was required to tap into my subconscious. I danced for the gods, if they were the larvae at the bottom of a mezcal bottle. At one point my body expected between two and five drinks a night, starting around six o'clock in the evening, which often meant having to choose between the gym or half a bottle of Bordeaux, between driving to a friend's house for dinner or muddling blueberries for a solo gin and tonic. On numerous occasions I've left dry parties early to go home and drink alone. There's something sublime about the way a glass of scotch steams up in the shower.

Some people, upon discovering the quantities at play, have told me, "Oh that's nothing. *That's* not alcoholism," as if we all have the same tolerances, the same measurements etched on our inner beakers. This kind of comparison is dangerous; so many people use it to rationalize habits they try to convince themselves aren't that bad. How does anyone else know how much of a substance blunts the clarity I need to function, to live my life and take care of those close to me? How does anyone know what number of beers is consistently too many to *just miss* something? No one can measure quantities for you.

I kept office hours at Snack N' Blues, a local bar with wall-to-wall Miles Davis posters, commedia dell'arte clowns suspended from the ceiling, and Coco, an eighty-year-old deejay from Madagascar who had a talent for syncing up live Rolling Stones albums with video projections of lizards fucking in a landscape he clearly missed. The highlight was the candy buffet. You could stuff your face with as many gummies and chocolate-covered almonds as you wanted—as long as you quaffed beer at a good clip. My access to the candy was never in danger.

In 2011, when I felt my writing career had stalled and that I was a failure as a novelist—based on criteria legible only to me—I drank even harder. It got worse when I lost my full-time job. I sat on the sofa with a flask and moped for a year. I sank deep into intoxication and numbness and lost perspective on myself and on what was going on around me. Perhaps I could have been a better brother, friend, partner, son. I *know* I could have. My partner Mark would suggest I drink less, or less often, which I would do for a spell, before

I would increase my intake again. Cutting down didn't work for me—my brain found a way to rationalize back to original quantities, using every possible loophole to get there. Then Mark and I would have the conversation all over again. I've apologized for subjecting him to this behaviour, for the helplessness he must have felt in those moments.

Mark had quit drinking over a decade before. My partner Wes, on the other hand, has never tried alcohol. They've never been bitten by the stiff wind of a neat Cutty Sark. They work in public health and have held a job in a hospital ER, where they've seen patients admitted for all sorts of illnesses, injuries, and abuses related to alcohol. I drank in front of them early in our relationship, but kissing them with beer breath eventually stopped making sense. Both Wes and Mark have been rock-solid supports in my struggles with alcohol. They've shown compassion without judgment. Several dear friends have done the same, some of whom have overcome—or are overcoming—addictions of their own.

———

When I was four, I hid in a kitchen cupboard and swigged from a bottle of red wine vinegar because I'd heard it would give me chin scruff. It pointedly did not, but now salads get me high.

———

In 2018, I decided to stop drinking altogether. I dismantled the wine rack in my bedroom and put it on the street, where someone picked it up within the hour, no doubt to set it up in another bedroom nearby.

The jonesing was hardest on days four and seventeen of my quitting. I could feel withdrawal curdle my blood and rake my last nerve. I grew irritable and restless, gritted my teeth and stared into space, looking for a way out of what I was feeling. I couldn't read or otherwise concentrate. Time lost meaning. Why days four and seventeen? I'll be trying to crack the numerology forever. It doesn't mean the other days were necessarily easier; the struggle was simply less noticeable.

After three months I started sleeping better. My sense of smell improved. I sniffed through the parks and alleys of Montreal and developed a potent new awareness of the city. I had less acid reflux, more joyous mornings, and better sex. Yay! There was also the unexpected upside of being able to drive at night, which is useful when you have friends who drink. There's nothing in the world quite like driving a drunk person who owns a car. They'll curse you for taking the wrong street even though you're literally saving their life. Then they'll thank you in the morning with little memory of the previous night's insults.

My relationship to Snack N' Blues changed along with my relationship to alcohol. When I went back with friends— so they could drink booze and I could drink soda—we suddenly weren't consuming enough for the owners, who complained we were freeloading too much candy. We walked out and never went back.

Throughout all this, one question robbed me of quiet: *Would I still be able to write?* Back when I was twenty-one and living in communal housing with six other bohemians, I smoked three packs of Gauloises *bleues* a day, kept the empty boxes, and glued them together to make a giant cigarette carton. It became our apartment's conversation piece. Now I realize it served as a statement—cubist and dangerous—that, by necessity, to produce art means to consume a substance, especially if you're using the art to telegraph pain. But there's a difference between the creative and the palliative, as Leslie Jamison points out in her essay "Does Recovery Kill Great Writing?": "If you needed to drink that much, you had to hurt, and drinking and writing were two different responses to that same molten pain: You could numb it, or you could grant it a voice."

There was no evidence that drinking had ever helped my writing career. In fact, my experience pointed to the contrary. There was the time a producer was waiting to see my synopsis for a short film so that he could submit it for a grant. I procrastinated on final revisions until the night before the deadline. Instead of devoting my mind fully to the delicate surgery, I slipped into a bottle of red and mucked through the task without a clue. Rejection is part of the game, but when we got the no, I knew it was because I'd chosen Cariñena grapes over nailing a moment that could change my life. The producer never called me again. The unmade film still plays in my head, the fifteen minutes now an endless script of what could have been.

Now I have to ask: What had booze done to my novels? I don't think I want to know the answer.

I did some of my best writing my first year sober. I could finally think clearly. I no longer needed to inhabit a stupor of soporifics and self-pity for text to flow. I could write during the day and continue at night, long past the time when alcohol used to make focus impossible. More importantly, I began to understand my life better. *That same molten pain.* I got perspective on why I'd started drinking in the first place, what had prompted me to self-medicate. The work wasn't easy. In my experience, pain doesn't lessen when you confront it.

———

Holding our liquor is a misnomer when we are the ones held.

———

I spent eighteen years in a group that taught me to hate myself. You cannot be queer and a Jehovah's Witness—it's one or the other. But for a while I was both, like being tied to a pair of jetliners taking off in opposite directions, a perfect way to get torn in two.

In the summer of 2018, the year I quit alcohol, I found out that Stephen, the tall, jokey congregation friend I hadn't seen in forever, had drunk himself to death after years of substance use and mental health issues linked to his own shunning. He was anathema to his family while alive; in death, they denied him a funeral. This was unimaginable to the new community he'd eventually found, a sprawl of house music deejays from all over. His music friends decided to throw him a final event, one last jam reverberating into the night. A party funeral: how fitting. I learned that Stephen was the dancer who'd held a scene together, who'd given his groupies—the cluster of friends who surpassed whatever the Witnesses once meant to him—an irresistible beat to keep time to. Stephen was reportedly always the last to leave the dance floor.

I hadn't expected to see so many of my old crew. Here we were in a bizarro version of our congregation, decades collapsed into a few minutes, a reckoning. We stared at one another, stunned and unsure what to say, using versions of our names that were dead to us. *Brother Cox.* We soon found the words and it started to feel natural; we fell into our rhythms. Natalya chatted with me as if nothing had happened between us. I wonder if she remembered my comment about her handsome boyfriend. Another friend and I compared text messages from our mothers, with their identical syntax and grammar of warning: Armageddon was coming and we should *return to the fold* while there was still time. Ian gave me a bear hug; he was hammered and offered me shots all night, even though I didn't drink. The irony of honouring, in a bar, someone who died of alcohol poisoning. Ian lectured me on the importance of living my life fully, which he'd been doing long before I did.

Then there was Danny, my ex-bandmate. He kept nuzzling my head and saying my name over and over, loudly then quietly. We were delirious to see each other again. When someone took the mic to speak about the connections between shunning, PTSD, depression, addiction, and suicide, Danny grabbed it out of their hands and yelled "Fuck religion!" before the MC cut him off, in an apparent disagreement over what the tone of the evening should be. How we use a microphone had been policed our entire lives, so it wasn't shocking for those dictums to continue here—even in a bar full of apostates.

So many of us had left *the truth*. We cried together and hugged hard to make up for the long physical absence. We were each broken in our own way. We moved to the basement of an adjacent club, where a candlelight shrine to Stephen was set up beside the dance floor; in the portrait of him, he was in his dopest clubwear. The deejays spun us around with thick Chicago and Detroit beats, old-school tracks everyone seemed to know. We took Stephen's photo and held it over our heads, touching him to the stars. People who'd been silent at the ceremony howled their rage under the strobes. There was something gospel about the beat, even heretic. The Witnesses don't believe in being born again, but that's exactly what happened to each of us gathered there. I let it all out.

Ian died a few months later, in a fog of unknown substances. First Stephen, then him. It was hard not to feel like the universe was fucking with me. Who's next? Would I be able to tell if accumulated pain was trying to kill me? I'm still trying to shake off that summer of death, the stench of flowers and embalming fluid.

———

I'm going to call a vodka cranberry with grenadine syrup a *Blood Transfusion* and recommend it to any Jehovah's Witness looking to stir things up.

———

I've gotten over the diplomat-grade coke I used to snort in New York with the U.N. caterer between his shifts serving canapés to Kofi Annan. Same with the ecstasy I ground up and snorted at circuit parties. Pot was slightly more attractive to me because of how my first roommate, Matt, packaged it. He was the first real friend I made after leaving the Witnesses.

At night he'd take me to the roof of our apartment building in Montreal's gay village, where we'd lie on a threadbare blanket and smoke while he introduced me to philosophy. Deleuze and Guattari was a way to rearrange the stars overhead; thinking critically like that made me realize how much work my brain could do in this lifetime. Matt spoke in a series of constellations, sprayed into a fine mist over our heads. We once dropped acid and watched a casserole of mac and cheese explode on the burner. Seeing glass and sauce fly in slow motion to all corners of the room was like witnessing the birth of a galaxy. Then we went downtown, where my ankle inexplicably got stuck in a revolving door and thirty people watched while Matt worked to free me, which I suppose he'd been doing in more ways than one.

Cigarettes were a different story. I smoked tobacco for ten years, managing to huff through most of a pack even when I was sick with bronchitis. One night in New York, when I had no money to get back to my place in the Bronx, I attempted to trade a pair of broken, lopsided sunglasses and a half-pack of Newport Menthols for subway fare, and when I couldn't interest anyone I slept on a pile of garbage bags until some Chelsea queens woke me up by shouting "How could anyone live like that!" I assumed, at the time, that they were referring to my choice of cigarette brand, a crystalline horror

of fibreglass and spearmint, which I believe I'm still cough-
ing from more than twenty years later. If I hadn't bought the
pack I would've had enough to take the subway.

I tried and failed to quit many times. Nicotine gum gave
me an illicit rush that felt like my heart was going to explode.
When I finally decided to try the Nicoderm patch, I'd have
to take it off to smoke after intense arguments with my ex.
Sometimes I'd stick it to my spine so that I could feel that
chemical course through my body more quickly. When
I called the Nicoderm helpline, they asked how long I'd been
using it. I told them eight months, and the person hung up.
I had blown past the suggested three-month period, and I
guess I was a liability.

———

The Jehovah's Witnesses claim to help people with addictions, as do many cultlike groups. They grow their numbers
by targeting those in trouble, and they use the language of
recovery—as well as a gentle but persistent love bombing—
to attract them, keying off a desire to be purified. Faults are
prayed away. But they offer judgment and scaremongering
instead of grief counselling and other types of mental
health support a person in recovery needs. Groups like

this want their acolytes free of substances, not so they can think critically, but so their minds can become containers for dogma, vessels for *the truth*. People might stick around solely because membership equals sobriety and backsliding on meetings could lead to relapse. I remember a carousel of people who suddenly showed up at the Kingdom Hall, some clearly on the downslope of benders or in withdrawal, in dirty jeans and T-shirts that stank of their vices. Sometimes they cleaned up and came back; other times we never saw them again.

For me, quitting drinking has meant hearing echoes of Witness-speak, the voices of those who once lectured us about clean living, that drinking was okay if it was done "in moderation." I've mostly avoided the language and structure of addiction recovery because it reminds me too much of Jehovah, and I've wanted to be sure my reasons for quitting aren't leftovers of my indoctrination. Here are the first three of the twelve steps of Alcoholics Anonymous: "We admitted we were powerless over alcohol—that our lives had become unmanageable." "Came to believe that a Power greater than ourselves could restore us to sanity." "Made a decision to turn our will and our lives over to the care of God as we understood Him." How could this last mantra ever serve people like me or Stephen, who'd probably first turned to drinking *because* of religion? Many have written about what it means for AA to tell generations of women that they must surrender power. For women in recovery with backgrounds in both subtly and overtly misogynist religions, what power is there left to surrender?

The twelve "traditions" also worry me. "Alcoholics Anonymous has no opinion on outside issues; hence the AA name ought never be drawn into public controversy." This language mirrors the Witnesses' being *no part of this world*, a stance that translates into not voting, protesting, or taking an interest in politics other than to comment on how it fulfills Bible prophecy. In other words, the JW brand of neutrality means tacit acceptance of the status quo and all its systemic harms. Is AA implying that it's happy to be a bystander in the face of injustice? Is the group completely free of accountability because outside standards don't apply?

Here's another one: "Anonymity is the spiritual foundation of all our traditions, ever reminding us to place principles before personalities." This sounds a lot like what JWs say about deferring all credit and glory to Jehovah, an extension of the idea that *the meek shall inherit the earth*. This statement has the effect of discouraging members from becoming authors and other creators with a stake in public intellectual life. *Be meek and shut the hell up. Your silence is worth more to us than your thoughts.*

These tactics extend beyond the world of substance use recovery. In his memoir *Boy Erased*, Garrard Conley reveals how gay conversion therapy, by framing queerness as a vice, uses the AA playbook to inflict violence on countless youth, deploying the language of care and concern to lure them into misplaced trust.

It's not always easy to find a secular path to recovery. There's often a church tie-in. For many, leaving a belief system behind means replacing it with another. Sometimes, when the timing is right and so is the vibe, a group can offer the type of spirituality or philosophy a person has been looking for their whole life. But when it happens right away, it strikes me as a rebound. I'm intrigued when a Witness leaves for another Christian group, yet another way to have their thoughts organized around a redemption narrative. Why not grift for a few years instead? An apostate might do well to define a vocabulary for themselves before adopting the lexicon of yet another ideology they didn't create. In my being judgmental like this, I'm forgetting that it can be hard to stay in the limbo between a life you've left and one you haven't built yet. And I'm forgetting that *I* left religion for another belief system, one replete with its own holy texts, cardinal rules, and hallowed saints: the church of books. The diverse manifestations of alcoholism and its treatment can be mystifying, even to those who seek solutions more rooted in a scientific basis than AA, which, in the end, may be as good a method as any. I'm glad recovery and addiction treatment programs are there for those who need them. I just wish that recovery doesn't become something else to recover from.

As for me, I'm grateful to everyone who helps lift me out of self-destructive behaviour with the lightest of touches—if a stronger touch isn't required. I'm thankful that they've let me define my own benchmarks and imagine my own futures. After my first sober year I intentionally started drinking again, but in lower quantities. Then when that no longer felt good, I quit again, and now I've been sober for over two years. I'm thankful that when I tell my friends I still think about alcohol every day—the smell of the cork, the sound of that first splash as it hits the bottom of the glass—they listen. They let me buy them wine because I can pick out a good one. Remembering is a drug I allow myself, and I'm not ashamed to say it.

REFERENDUM NIGHT

If you were to take a walk in Montreal in October 1995, you would feel the bite of the fall air. Love and disagreement—which are not opposites—would surround you in a variety of languages. You would see cultural and linguistic play intertwined, and you'd also see nationalism attempt to erase it. You would feel divisions, long obscured, become more obvious, thickening like frost over everything. In the months leading up to the referendum over whether Quebec should separate from Canada—whatever separation means, whatever *Canada* means—the vote wasn't exactly something you could discuss with co-workers, classmates, or even with every friend. We often pretended that language didn't separate us from one another, sometimes as a way to keep the peace. Something that Quebec shares with Canada is the lethal politesse of white supremacy—the smiling silence of it all.

That fall, the city was a patchwork of blue *Oui* and red *Non* signs, of evolution and stagnancy, of poverty and the stench of old money, of self-determination and federalism, of English oppression and francophone independence, of two solitudes ignoring Indigenous realities and other third solitudes all over the land. It had been just five years since the Kanesatake Resistance, also known as the Oka Crisis, when Kanien'kehá:ka (Mohawk) protesters held off the police and the army for seventy-eight days in the wake of a plan to expand a golf course and build townhouses over ancestral burial grounds in an area known as the Pines, lands that the government has never deemed worthy of protection for the Kanien'kehá:ka. After the standoff ended the development never went forward, but uncertainty and tension stuck around like a mist that had still not lifted by referendum night.

In 1995, we were reduced from a plurality to a binary. Immigrants and other allophones were made to feel unsafe, and as unwanted obstacles to freedom for millions. Lucien Bouchard, one of the charismatic entrepreneurs of the Parti Québécois, ripped into Canada for consistently throwing the province under the bus, no doubt one of the buses that

Prime Minister Chrétien authorized to bring in Canadians from other provinces for displays of flag-waving, federalist love, a perhaps illegal attempt to sway the vote. Later, when Bouchard survived flesh-eating bacteria despite losing a leg, many took it as a miracle, a sign of the second coming of René Lévesque, the father of the Quebec sovereigntist movement who continued to whisper freedom into the hearts of mostly francophone Quebecers from Cimetière Saint-Michel de Sillery, burial grounds that were allowed to be hallowed. A few anglophones pushed for sovereignty as an act of anti-federalist sentiment. That October, one could hear Gilles Vigneault, Robert Charlebois, and Beau Dommage blast out of speakers at impromptu backyard barbecues to prematurely celebrate the rupture. The rapture? The air held the electricity of change, of something coming. It was both a crackle and a smell. Ottawa had fucked us all over—some of us more than others—and now they were going to get it.

What is the question? Good question.

Do you agree that Quebec should become sovereign, after having made a formal offer to Canada for a new economic and political partnership, within the scope of the bill respecting the future of Quebec and of the agreement signed on June 12, 1995?

We didn't know what this meant then, and it's still unclear. Become a sovereign *what*? And exactly *what* partnership? The writers of the referendum question wrote it in secret. Isn't that how it always goes? Within this inscrutable question, a million more bloomed. Would we keep our own currency, and if not, who would be on the money? We suspected but didn't name anyone. Would we have our own military? When I explained the referendum and the aims of the Parti Québécois to friends in Croatia, they asked, "How do you expect to have a revolution without bloodshed?" And it's true. It was later revealed that the federal government had no plans to recognize a *Oui*, and in that event, Quebec would have proceeded with a unilateral declaration of independence. Of course Canada would declare the secession illegal; why would a colonial government voluntarily cede its power that way? That's exactly what the Watch Tower Society does to members who leave or try to: declare invalid whatever life they can build on the outside, declare them deserving of death at Armageddon, declare them already dead. If you're part of a group that's impossible to leave, you should never have been part of it in the first place.

But there's another conversation here. The unceded lands that Canada and Quebec sit on are heavy with the history of colonial genocide. Even under the guise of peace, any further redrawing of the map by white people could not erase that violence from memory. It would simply be another form of land clearing. Where would a referendum result leave the Indigenous people in what is now Quebec and their right to self-determination? What about sovereignty for Tiohtià:ke, gathering place for many First Nations and home of the Kanien'kehá:ka? Why didn't we hear much about the Cree referendum on Quebec sovereignty on October 24, 1995, or the one held by Inuit on October 29, what was asked and not asked, what was answered and left unsaid, or even how the votes went?

What is the question? Good question.

Would we need passports to cross into Ontario? What countries would recognize a Quebec passport, and what colour would it be, since Canada's is already blue? What does a bluer blue look like? Is azure a nationalist colour? When Bill Clinton gave a public address praising Canadian unity five days before the vote, how were we supposed to react? When queer men fucked in bathhouses, what official languages would we use? The primal exchange that happens during sex is a microcosm of communication. What do you say to someone you're fucking when you realize mid-orgasm that they voted the other way? Maybe we could fuck the question into oblivion and we wouldn't need answers.

I watched all this from the mostly anglophone suburb of Pierrefonds, whose residents would vote almost overwhelmingly *Non*. But electoral ridings would not decide the outcome of this one. Referendums in Quebec are decided by popular vote. Every vote counts—what a strange concept.

The year of the referendum, I was newly out of the Jehovah's Witnesses. I was nineteen and of legal voting age in Quebec. In theory, I could choose to count myself among what would end up to be the largest voter turnout in Quebec history. I was raised in a group that taught me to be "politically neutral"—as if to do nothing was to be apolitical. Humans supposedly have zero power in this wicked system because Satan is in charge, so a final vote tally couldn't possibly matter. We were told that either way—*Oui* or *Non*—it was pointless: only God could govern correctly, and he would abolish all political systems at Armageddon, which was coming any day now. Until the final judgment, elections were merely distractions from the important work of storing treasures in heaven. "We obey God by not favoring any politician or political group, even when their ideas or opinions could benefit us," says *The Watchtower*. "If we want to remain neutral, we should avoid feeling that one side is right or is better than another." It's a recipe for maintaining systemic oppression in all its forms.

One study shows that over a quarter of Jehovah's Witnesses in America are Black and almost a third are Latinx, but the group's hierarchy has almost always been exclusively white. In 2020, the week George Floyd was murdered by a cop, the lead article on JW.org suggested passivity and silence: "Although some protesters may accomplish their aims, God's Kingdom offers a better solution." What the Witnesses don't understand is that if Armageddon *does* come and they survive it, systemic racism will survive along with them, because it's baked into their policies and practices. In the meantime, Witnesses of colour have to fight for their very lives, and they have to do it either alone or with the help of people they're forbidden from associating with.

What better way to rebut *The Watchtower* than to cast my first vote, almost as if it mattered?

On referendum day, October 30, I was proud to take my voter ID card to the high school gymnasium turned polling station. It was certainly the pride of Satan. There was hardly anyone in line—no one to see me cross the long expanse of the gym to the cardboard booth, pick up a pencil, and make my choice. At the time, I was unaware of the irony of voting against political independence within a year of my acquiring it.

Would I have voted secretly even if I hadn't officially left the Witnesses by referendum day? Good question.

After I cast my ballot, I went home and turned on the news. I don't know if my mother knew where I'd been earlier that day. We watched the broadcast for different reasons: she to take in a political system that would soon be replaced by a Witness theocracy; I to see whether my vote had any discernible effect. We waited as the tally hovered within the margin of a single percentage point. Maybe my vote would be the difference. The city, the province, the country were on edge. The anchors were stressed, and so were supporters at both campaign headquarters—faces contorted by anguish, hope, fear, uncertainty. The *Non* side won, just barely, but it didn't feel like a victory. The *Oui* side flipped out, history denied to them. In his concession speech, Jacques Parizeau, premier of Quebec and torchbearer for what he was certain would be a historic night, blamed the loss on "*l'argent et des votes ethniques*," and resigned the following day. His comment was widely mistranslated as "the ethnic vote" instead of "ethnic votes," as if, within the linguistic nuances between them, the sovereigntist dream could be made to encompass the people it was always meant to exclude. As if, in the end, we had not all lost.

But I was still emboldened from having held that pencil. The key to writing a good question is wrestling with it. What is the question? Good question.

> *Do you agree that Daniel should exercise his independent politi-*
> *cal will, after having made a formal offer to himself for a new*
> *relationship to spirituality and the authorities who claim to*
> *adjudicate it, within the scope of the bill respecting his future,*
> *and of the agreement signed with Satan the Devil on the day*
> *Daniel disassociated from the Jehovah's Witnesses?*

THE END OF TIMES SQUARE

Most people—especially those who live in cities—if they look over the important occurrences in their lives over a substantial period of time, will likely notice that a substantial number of the important or dramatic ones, material or psychological, first arrived through strangers encountered in public spaces.

—SAMUEL R. DELANY, *TIMES SQUARE RED, TIMES SQUARE BLUE*

In 1998, halfway through my failed undergrad stint, I decided to spend a week in New York. I got off the bus at Port Authority, bunked in a hostel in Chelsea, and cruised the local bodegas, amazed by a city where watermelon came cubed. I memorized the unique scent mixture of sewer, garbage, and flower bouquets in case I never came here or smelled it again, or in case I needed the trail to find my way back.

I decided to close out my week at Beige, the famous Tuesday night party on the Bowery, where I'd heard that the demimonde of Lower Manhattan came out to play. I palmed a bottle of Rolling Rock and let the green glass sweat in my hand as I smoked in a corner of the outdoor patio in a jean jacket whose sleeves I'd cut with scissors before my trip. The place was packed, and I had no choice but to mingle. Soon enough, a guy started talking to me: big smile, longish hair, in jeans and a chic top. A trucker hat completed the look. We chatted a bit. I don't remember much of what we talked about, but he probably asked what I was doing there. He had a big entourage—maybe ten or fifteen people who laughed at all his jokes. "David! That's hilarious. Did you hear what David said?" At one point, one of his friends came over to me. "You have no idea who he is, do you?" I didn't. And I also had no idea how refreshing that could be to him. We took a cab back to his East Village apartment, which was covered in art prints and blown-up photos. When we crawled into bed I couldn't stop staring at the diorama of Duran Duran on the folding wood screen that took up half the room.

I had just unknowingly spent the night with David LaChapelle, the pop artist and fashion photographer who famously took the last-ever portrait of his mentor Andy Warhol. David was known for his colour-drenched celebrity photos and music videos that created a new aesthetic out of the unconventional, the banal, the grotesque. Nearly every project of his is a master lesson in how to worship at the church of Late Capitalism, as worn and consumed by a diversity of bodies rejected by the mainstream beauty industry, with an iconography all his own.

I only found this out after I took the bus back to Montreal and talked about David with my roommates, one of whom knew all about him. "Unbelievable. You're a starfucker." Did it count if I didn't know who he was? I took this as a sign that New York was a good place for me to be. So a few months later, I dropped out of university and decided to move there.

———

When I got off the bus in New York for the second time, I didn't have much more in my backpack than I'd taken on my trip the year before. Nor did I have a job lined up or anywhere to live, but I wasn't too worried about it. I had thirteen hundred dollars in cash in my pocket and believed I was rich. If I needed to spend a few nights in a hotel, so be it.

I stepped out onto Eighth Avenue and took in the speed, the noise, the heat, the way the city closes in on you in summer. I knew very little about the history of the avenue.

At some point I'd internalized the cliché that New York was the ultimate challenge for a young artist, a proving ground. It's white privilege not to *need* to be somewhere yet to still go there and assume you'll land safely; to live with the illusion of having no responsibilities. I hadn't even researched the obstacles that lay ahead of me.

I hauled ass to the Big Cup coffee shop in Chelsea, and when I wasn't flirting with the local boys—who had a fascination with my wheeled luggage, what it might contain, and what my itinerancy said about their prospects of getting me into bed—I flipped through *The Village Voice*, where I saw an ad for an apartment rental agency. I went to the agency office and chose a room in Crown Heights, Brooklyn, based on Polaroids in a binder. I had no idea how far the neighbourhood was from Manhattan, nor that I would spend every second in my rented room plotting my way back to the city.

In those days hundred-dollar bills practically blew down New York City avenues, so I figured a few were bound to come my way. I fell into a job shuttling furniture I could never afford across the five boroughs. One day when I was loitering downtown after a move, a guy rode up to me on a bicycle, told me I was handsome and should be a model if I wasn't already, and handed me a business card. He was a photographer. A few days later I was lathering up in a

Williamsburg shower while he snapped photos through the glass panes. I hadn't spent much time online by then, but I knew the internet was a thing and that I would be part of it. One shower scene led to another, and soon I was the cleanest boy in the city, and supposedly on the World Wide Web.

Photographers traded my beeper number and I was never not busy. One of them, Misa, scheduled a shoot with me and another guy, Shane, for *Honcho*, a monthly skin mag for connoisseurs of scruff, cigars, and spit-shined leather. There was room for boys like us with profusions of chest and pit hair that otherwise betrayed our twinkdom. *Honcho* was artsy and encouraged contributors to take risks of representation and genre. Every issue featured erotica, illustrated fiction, visual art, interviews with kinksters, classified ads, and full-page spreads that could make the Marquis de Sade blush. Professional escorts gave tips on how to pack supplies for a perfect night of tricking.

Misa proposed we shoot at the Gavin Brown Gallery on West 14th Street, which was hosting an installation at the time, one that consisted of a lifelike apartment with the artist supposedly living in it, and where visitors could squat for as long as they liked. *Were we all right with posing nude in public? Of course!* It was an insult to even ask. I pushed Shane's face

into my half-hard cock while leaning against a plywood wall
graffitied as follows:

M	O	M	A
U	F	Y	S
S			S
E			
U			
M			

Could anyone have given us a better imprimatur?
Whoever wrote that had no way of knowing how well we
would embody the sentiment; how I would thrust my hand
through the waistband of Shane's tighty-whities and out a
leg hole, lift him up and tear the fabric wedgie-style while
flipping the bird for the camera, then hold the pose to turn
us into a statue. I'd like to think it was the art that got and
kept me hard. Someone lay on a pile of pillows in a little
enclosure a few feet away, and to this day I have no idea if it

was the artist, a gallery employee, or a visitor. I suppose it doesn't matter; either way, we were doing performance art. The divisions between art and porn—as tools to separate factions of society in order to better control them—had been torn away, at least for the afternoon.

It didn't occur to me that one day photos of me would hang in galleries, but I was aware of the political context of doing sex work and doing it as publicly as possible. This was the New York of Rudy Giuliani. He wanted to keep the city sexless, defang performance art, and render our hangout spaces anodyne. The Forty-second Street Development Project meant that in 1995—just a few years before I arrived in the city—zoning laws had shuttered the Capri, the Venus, the Eros, and other porn theatres in Times Square, a continuation of how the Office of Midtown Enforcement had closed hundreds of massage parlours, strip clubs, bookstores that carried smut, and peep shows throughout the 1980s and 90s. Money was the reason and AIDS and crime were the excuses. Some of these businesses, if not closed, were "relocated" to the West Side along the Hudson River to make way for the corporate takeover of the city's cultural centre. Members of queer and trans communities who are multiply marginalized—including people of colour, HIV-positive people, and sex workers acting with less agency than I did—had never been safe in these spaces when they were in Times Square, and were even less safe once these establishments were pushed west, further to the margins.

In 1999 the Brooklyn Museum of Art put on an exhibit from the U.K. called *Sensation*, which featured, among other works, erotic photos of a couple taken by their son, animals suspended in formaldehyde, and a Black Madonna spackled with elephant manure. The Mayor's Office threatened to pull the museum's funding unless it closed the show. Giuliani called it "sick stuff," saying that "if you want to throw dung at something—I could figure out how to do that." It's uncanny how prophetic his proclivity for shit was: his later defence and enablement of the Trump administration in its attempts to sabotage democracy is far more obscene than the experiments of young British artists.

When City Hall cracked down on cruising, you couldn't fuck in the bushes in Central Park anymore; the person you would proposition could be a cop with a hard-on for seeing you in jail. In that respect, "Forty-second Street Development Project" is a misnomer. It was actually a project to develop the *entire city* in order to make straight white families, including tourists, feel more comfortable spending money, which meant erasing expressions of queer sex from public view. "One is reminded of seventeenth-century London and

Marseille's response to the plague—though here the plague may just be that pleasant suburban couple, lawyer and doctor, herding their 2.3 children ahead of them, out the door of the airport van and into the Milford Plaza; or at least the family values, perhaps too easily, they might be taken by some to represent," writes Samuel R. Delany in *Times Square Red, Times Square Blue*. It was a battle for the soul of the city, and New York queers fought back. At the time, I was mostly unaware of ACT UP artmaking as a tradition of resistance to Giuliani and the mayors before him over their inadequate and harmful responses to the AIDS crisis, so I didn't know how what we were doing might borrow from and echo that work.

In another spread for *Honcho*, Misa shot me and Sox, a performer I'd done a film with and had a crush on. We posed in the Central Park bushes—evidence of us breaking the law—to make a point. Let me clarify that no one could see us. We weren't exposing ourselves to anybody without their consent. Sox and I snaked between the spiky branches and pulled our underwear down to give the camera a good look. We were furtive flashers and jerked each other off a bit before we scattered. Who knew when a cop would crawl out of the shrubs covered in dog shit and brandishing a badge? Did we have an overblown sense of self-importance regarding our mission? Of course. There was no piece of fabric big enough to contain the bulge of our collective ego.

We horny young queers resisted Giuliani on many aesthetic fronts. *Nerve* magazine came out with a piece on the confluence of art and porn and we said *Oui*—the way to keep the culture from closing shut was to keep our assholes wide open to possibility. This melding of high brow and smut was real. Photographers were freer to work without the pressure of having to distinguish between the modes so starkly. For years they'd proven that a photo dripping in sex could hang both in a sex club and in a gallery. It's an erotic experience to commune with a work of visual art, in search of a private conversation just outside the spray of track lighting. Maybe it was the Golden Age of the Sapiosexual.

Bruce LaBruce, the Canadian queercore icon, had been making this case for years in his films *No Skin Off My Ass, Super 8½,* and *Hustler White.* LaBruce finds ever new ways to scandalize festival audiences, simply by pointing to the gap between their pretensions and their desires. I've seen him rewrite a script on the fly to recalibrate the mix of low glam and high camp. The result is a cinéma-vérité style that blends tones in a way not every critic can handle, probably because it pokes holes in the walls between the genres they're expected to uphold. LaBruce does the same work in his sacrilegious photography, which once got an art gallery in Madrid bombed, the ruins, strangely, looking like the set of his film *The Raspberry Reich*. In 1999 I went to a screening of one of his movies in the East Village hosted by a LaBruce impersonator, unaware that I'd one day collaborate with and befriend the real thing, and that in Venice I'd get to witness him scandalize film critics who had to let their expectations sink into the algae blooms of the lagoon.

I spread my legs and thought of Giuliani. I thought of him and his army of arrest-happy cops when I scaled a fence at Riverside Park with Richard Kern so that he could shoot me with rat traps dangling from my foreskin for *Inches* magazine. I thought of the mayor when I smashed a plaster pillar and photographer Reed Massengill posed me over shards that threatened to puncture my scrotum. *This*, I thought, *is how we hustlers will remake New York from scratch*. I thought of the mayor when I pounded ass on my first Viagra high, digging into the sofa cushions for lube. I thought of the mayor when I was sprawled shirtless on the floor of Stanley Stellar's studio with a notebook and a pen, unsure how to tell my story while I was acting it out on camera.

———

With the rush to accommodate the new, much that was beautiful along with much that was shoddy, much that was dilapidated with much that was pleasurable, much that was inefficient with much that was functional, is gone. The idea that all that is going was ugly and awful is as absurd as it would be to propose that what was there was only of any one moral color.

—SAMUEL R. DELANY, *TIMES SQUARE RED, TIMES SQUARE BLUE*

———

After I'd been settled in New York for a few months, David took me for soup at Café Orlin in the East Village. I told him what I'd been up to in the city, my photo shoots and the constant grind to find new work. In case I still wasn't sure who he was, he gave me a copy of the latest issue of *The Advocate* that had him on the cover, shirtless and in red boxing gloves, sitting in the corner of a ring, his face faux bruised and scuffed. The interview was about his life and career, and a rather public spat he was having with Mira Sorvino. The fact that he was a cover boy impressed me. *I could be a cover boy too*, I thought.

We hung out at his studio on East 13th Street about once a month. It usually followed a script. I would ring the bell, David's assistant would buzz me in, and I would walk up the two flights and come face to face with the ceramic leopards that David had shot Elton John with. Sometimes I waited awhile for David to be free. Eventually he'd mosey out in a white track suit to talk to me, distracted by staff who asked him questions constantly. I must've been a nuisance, bugging him like that in the middle of his workdays, time he could've better spent shooting Eminem and Bowie and Leonardo for *Vogue* and *Spin* and *Rolling Stone*.

The studio was a zoo, an idea and culture factory of Warholian proportions. The props room was a funhouse of the darkest parts of the American psyche. Stylists in New York don't walk, they fly, because they have to find the impossible in all five boroughs—and sometimes New Jersey. And if it doesn't exist, they have to create it. Giant inflatable lips sat deflated in a corner. There was a life-size plaster mould of Michelangelo's David, which was kind of a joke, because now there were *two* Davids made in God's image. Or maybe the joke was that David was the new Michelangelo, turning ordinary celebs into deities. Makeup artists emptied bags of lipstick tubes on the floor to look for the perfect shade for Amanda Lepore to wear to the club that night. Scriptwriters from L.A. typed furiously in corners and pitched ideas to David whenever he walked by. The studio was a factory of American culture. Warhol would've been proud, or at least intrigued.

I didn't know it at the time, but David shot Michael Jackson twice: once in 1998 for *Flaunt*, and again in 1999 for *Rolling Stone*. This would continue my tradition of near misses with MJ. I clearly hadn't visited the studio on the right days.

When we danced at loft parties together, people shot me jealous looks. That's when I truly understood how others saw David: "the Fellini of photography," as one journalist had put it. A modern Magritte, and the most in-demand surrealist of our generation. What was the endgame of it all? This kind of fantasy wasn't meant to last forever.

———

The morning my first *Honcho* cover was due to come out, I lined up at dawn at the curbside newsstand at the corner of Houston and Broadway, the one under the DKNY fresco, you couldn't miss it. I wanted to get the first copy. I was on the cover all right, but I was disappointed when I looked through my open zipper and saw that my pubes had been airbrushed off—leaving them on would've incurred the extra expense of shrink wrap to conform to new laws governing "family fare" and what could and couldn't be displayed openly in public. It's strange how I wasn't more disturbed that I appeared in army fatigues and was wrapped in Old Glory, and that Giuliani would go on to militarize the city—and the nation—using these same emblems.

———

My boyfriend Broc knew I shucked pants for gay porn magazines and that my furry ass was plastered all over the city. He was fine with this. If he tried to rescue me, it wasn't from hustling but rather from the unthinkable tragedy of living in the Bronx, where I'd moved after a year of living in Crown Heights. Every few weeks he brought up the topic of my moving in with him, and every few months he mentioned sponsoring me to get a visa. There were a few problems with this proposal. Sponsor me to do *what*? I couldn't imagine writing *spreading my cheeks* on the immigration form.

It's easy to talk to boyfriends about porn when you both do it. I met one of them on set, and we couldn't wait to steal away for some private fucking. Other boyfriends were downright hostile to the idea. One of them took me to 2001 Odyssey, the disco in *Saturday Night Fever*, where we danced on the alternating colour blocks of the original dance floor. He told me I had to choose between him and porn. I scheduled another shoot a week later and left his ass in Brooklyn.

If someone asks you to stop doing what you love, dance with someone else.

There's something I never properly explained to my boyfriends: I wasn't doing sex work because it was my only option, I was doing it partly because—in my particular circumstances—it freed me. My reasons were similar to those of Mattilda Bernstein Sycamore. "When I first started turning tricks it was so I could make art and do activism and survive as far from mainstream consumerist norms as possible, that was all," she writes in *The Freezer Door*. "Suddenly I was all alone—there were only a few other hookers who even admitted what they did for a living, but they said they were doing it as a career. I'd chosen to be a hooker so I didn't have to have a career."

I believed that in my relationships I was on an even footing, with no financial dependencies. But when you're a hustler, it's only a matter of time before you stumble into a relationship so nebulous that you don't know what it is. I crashed with a painter named Patrick in a Chelsea loft that would cost tens of thousands a month today. He slept through the mornings and spent his afternoons shepherding two turtles across canvases with uncapped markers he strapped to their backs; this was how art was produced on the West Side. He didn't pay for the place, or for the gourmet turtle food from the Chelsea Market, or for the daffodils that lined the sunny windows. He had a sugar daddy, an art director for *Vanity Fair* who liked to fuck us both. Was he my daddy, too? All I wanted was a place to sleep in Manhattan—a convenient alternative to returning to my room in the Bronx when the night grew long—but it was clear I could've gotten much more if I'd asked for it.

Was I even a hustler? "By general consensus, a hustler is someone who sets a price beforehand and, if the payment is not agreed to, no encounter takes place," writes Delany, who goes on to trouble the line between commercial and non-commercial sex. "What of the encounter that starts off particularly well, so that one person pauses and says, 'Hey, I'm going to go out and get some sandwiches and a couple of cans of beer. I'll be back in ten minutes. What kind of sandwich you want? This way we can make an afternoon of it,' and is told, 'Great, man. Bring me a ham and cheese on rye with mustard.' Is that commercial?"

This is not to say I had *zero* business acumen when it came to sex work. One day my pager beeped with an unfamiliar number, so I called it back from a pay phone. It was a trick who'd seen me in *Honcho* and had asked around for my digits. I met him in the lobby of a hotel in Midtown, where he gave a fake name to the clerk. "Just to be clear, this is a touch-baser," he said to me in the room. "This is not the encounter per se, I just want to see if I like you." He wasn't planning to pay me. I could feel a scam coming on, so I pushed back. "How do I know I'll ever see you again?" He seemed offended—I'm sure he saw himself as the epitome of reliability. "It's just fifteen minutes. This is just a formality." I went along with the idea and did my time.

I must've passed the audition because he paged me a few weeks later. This time he was already waiting in the hotel room. A mint copy of my issue of *Honcho* lay on the desk. "I only fuck cover boys. Can you sign it?" I obliged. (How far I'd come from being a young Jehovah's Witness distributing *The Watchtower* magazine, when no one asked me to sign anything.) There was also an unopened bottle of vodka, three crisp hundred-dollar bills, and a dime bag of coke, all fastidiously laid out for me. What did this guy do for a living? I thought three hundred was a lot of money. We had sex and took breaks to do coke, smoke Newport Menthols, and watch infomercials. It was a perfectly curated boredom. But afterward, the trick seemed upset. I didn't think I'd done anything wrong. I had indulged all his peccadilloes and stayed rock hard. I asked him what the matter was. "I want my escorts to party with me. You weren't doing enough coke." Some men can never be pleased.

——

I thought of Giuliani when I did a raunch scene in *Brooklyn Meat Packers* with Donnie Russo, a BDSM porn icon who lived in the apartment above a funeral parlour his family owned and where he did makeup on corpses. How much piss could a foreskin hold if a foreskin could hold piss? Looking back, it's the pinnacle of bad 90s video production. Nothing's in focus and the pixels are bigger than cumshots. When Donnie's boyfriend Aaron Cobbett—a photographer whose hustler glam the Chelsea galleries couldn't get enough of—put me in boxing gloves, a navy and orange bomber jacket open to my bare chest, and great gobs of pancake makeup and lipliner, I may have thought of the closeted cops who might jerk off over the shots when they appeared in a German art book, pining over the escorts who got away. And wearing the boxing gloves, I may also have thought of David.

This is the portrait I mailed to my mom to let her know how I was doing. Don't ask me why. When I eventually returned to Canada, I found it framed in one of her bookcases.

——

I've tried to write about all this before. I wanted to show people that there was a brain in this body in case they forgot. I put it in a screenplay because I wanted to see the events projected in larger proportions than they had occurred. Does it seem I had my life together? It was a mess and so was the script. Maybe a film editor could make sense of the splices. Maybe a soundtrack would move me to be more compassionate toward some of the characters.

I Xeroxed a stack of scripts at a copy shop in Chelsea. Perfect-bound with a glue spine, kind of like me. I threw on a Kermit-green suit from a thrift store and brought my wares to production companies in the tower at 666 Broadway. I told the confused staff who let me in that my screenplay was the best film since *Buffalo '66*. It was the new *Blair Witch Project*. Maybe we could attach John Cameron Mitchell. I gave them the fax number of the copy shop, which I visited every day for a month to check for messages. They charged me a dollar every time, even though nothing ever came. It was official: I was hustling to subsidize my life as an artist. I eventually stopped visiting the copy shop, so I don't know if my greenlight ever spooled through the fax machine. It's just as well. If I'd spent half as much time revising as I'd spent on the subway getting to Chelsea every day, my screenplay might've been less terrible.

I also tried to write about some of this in my novel *Shuck*, but it didn't all come out right. I crafted a narrator who was just removed enough from me to create plausible deniability. I used the smokescreen of fiction to obscure memoir, which was most of it. When given a chance to clarify in interviews, I evaded. I became Jaeven, my novel's protagonist. I started to tell his stories and forgot parts of my own. Together, we came out too clean, each other's decoy and alibi. It was a narrative I'd found too easily, one of those narratives we tell ourselves so often that we forget to question them, to peel them back to find the truer ones. Maybe I'd tackled the material too early, before it had had time to simmer. Whatever the case, not everything about the way I handled dimensions of memoir in fiction at the time was ethical. I'm just starting to undo those mistakes. The cover of *Shuck* is a photo of a boy submerged in a bathtub, fully clothed. I have no idea who the model is, and it's fitting; even if it were me, I wouldn't have recognized myself.

———

"Do you go to the gym?" I was asked all the time. I was no Chelsea gym queen—I got my workouts on the moving vans. We met for shape-up in Vinegar Hill, Brooklyn, every morning before the boss would assign the crews and send us out. Our customers were mostly the Upper East Side types who would normally hire me for other reasons. I carted antiques up and down the avenues to develop my biceps and triceps, flirted with the doormen, and went shirtless in the cab pressed against two or three straight guys on the hottest of days. When I moved furniture I didn't think about porn at all; I thought about Tetris, how it all fit together. One of the companies I worked for was called Rainbow Movers, and some customers were visibly disappointed when they learned we weren't all the type of movers our name implied.

The wealthiest customers were never there to greet us— they had people to do that. On one job in a multi-floor brownstone, a cute young house manager started hitting on me right away. He asked what else I did, and I told him about my work in porn. Before too long he invited me to an empty floor upstairs. Some brownstones are so big they'll never be filled. This is the nature of wealth. There isn't enough furniture in Manhattan to do the job. We made good use of the space, he and I. Sometimes it's tricky to know who's getting a freebie in situations like this, or who's tipping who, or who's the customer and who's providing the service. Sometimes it feels like everything at once.

Some time later, I did a porn shoot where I posed as a mover showing up at someone's house all sweaty and horny. The spread appeared with a ridiculous interview, where under "Favourite thing to do" I answered "Women." I was out to many of my colleagues on the trucks, so I'm not sure what I gained by playing a closeted version of myself on camera. Maybe it had something to do with acting or messing with expectations. Maybe I was playing the mover I'd been when I worked at the family moving company: an alpha male who could never be suspected.

———

Whenever I crossed the Brooklyn Bridge I could see the Watch Tower marquees that loomed over the East River on the Brooklyn side, the ones that faced the atheist Towers of Babel in Manhattan and flashed neon messages that admonished residents to "Read God's Word" when they really meant their own interpretation of it. If I'd moved to New York to escape the Witnesses, I'd come to the wrong place.

Growing up a Jehovah boy, I heard a lot about the Great Harlot, the Whore of Babylon. In Watch Tower literature, false religion—which is any religion other than the JWs— is represented as a "prostitute," a lustful woman who "sleeps with the kings of the earth." The state will bed the church before finally devouring it, the story goes. Jehovah will kill false religion at Armageddon by turning the United Nations against it. The larger message is that having political affiliations made you a slut, a whore worthy of death. I later must have flipped this logic around to understand that turning tricks and stripping in front of the camera was a political act, regardless of whether it had anything to do with resisting Giuliani policies.

I saw my chance to become one of the villainous archetypes depicted in Witness literature and took it. If I knew I was going to die at Armageddon anyway, what did I have to lose? And I was a pretty slutty boy to begin with. Maybe I'd also internalized the idea that if being queer had *mostly* propelled me out of the Witnesses, this porny hyper-manifestation of that queerness was sure to complete the job. The Witnesses consider sex work such a grave sin that those practising it should either be rescued, condemned, or both—the conditions under which it occurs deserve no investigation. Sure enough, my family came across an interview I'd done with a Montreal weekly about my work in porn, and they made sure I knew their displeasure.

———

The thing about growing up in a doomsday cult is that it's always the end of the world. In 1999 the whispers of a new apocalypse started down by South Ferry, then moved along Wall Street, becoming louder as they shivered up Broadway and through Union Square on their inevitable glide uptown. People shut their windows but it was too late—the whispers had already gotten inside. The Y2K bug crept up on us: computer systems would misread the double zeroes of 2000 as 1900 and fry everything we'd built. Lazy coding in the 1960s and 70s would do us in. We couldn't bear the thought of the city blinking off and not coming back on again. To contemplate complete darkness is to embrace it, to give oneself over to the ravages of nothingness.

We were facing the death of America Online—not the company, but the concept. I was new to the net, so I didn't fully understand the impact. I'd walk up the six flights to my friend Hyram's apartment in the East Village to use his computer to type up interviews for *New York Waste*, a punk tabloid that printed my first bylines. I'd take breaks to surf. I was mystified by hyperlinks and spent afternoons clicking one blue underline after another. Apparently, this system could vanish when the power grid went *poof*. Technicians were working on the bug, which had never been a bug but rather a shortcut; Y2K preparedness became a thing, then that thing became a business—*so* New York. The millennium timer on the side of the Virgin Records building ticked us ever closer, but there was nothing to do, so we stopped looking up.

Maybe it wouldn't be that bad, I began to think. Midnight was for starting over. Prison doors would swing open and people would get second chances. Automated tellers would dispense bills to whoever needed them. Substandard school records would be expunged, including my own. The unearthly orange sunsets over the tailing ponds in the Meadowlands just across the water in New Jersey would replace the neons of Times Square and mark a return to nature. There was so much upside to the end of civilization.

When a couple from Chelsea I'd hooked up with invited me to move into a geodesic dome in Arizona they were planning to buy with their cashed-out savings, I said no. Even though logistically Y2K was the most plausible Armageddon I'd ever encountered, it was one of the few ends of the world I wasn't afraid of. Not so for Tara Westover's father, whom she describes in *Educated* as stockpiling food, fuel, and guns to weather what he assumed would be a resulting ten-year famine. Similarly, in *Interior States*, Meghan O'Gieblyn explains how her fundamentalist family hoarded so many freeze-dried rations to prepare for the millennium bug that they were eating the chalky leftovers until 2008.

Despite the expectation of doom, I was gleeful on New Year's Eve, 1999. I hadn't tagged along with any of my friends on their fancy, ticketed party plans. I was alone and happy about it. I went to a cramped East Village bar and danced with a small cluster of strangers. There was the lawyer whose glasses I stole for a few Kool & the Gang numbers; I bobbed and sloshed my vodka cranberry as I watched the ABC broadcast on the overhead television through lenses that gave me a headache for the ages, which was fine, because it was one I wanted to remember. You knew it was the end of the world when you saw Peter Jennings playing cards with his co-hosts; all hands turned over, nothing left to hide. I was pulled out the door before the song could finish, sucked out by my own wanderlust, and I walked uptown as if I were on the long-promised but still-absent Second Avenue Subway line, travelling north with thousands of half-drunk people. I was relatively sober. I didn't want to miss any of the hard, blunt realities of the night, good or bad. I wanted to be clear-minded enough to offer a short doxology to what I'd become that year—the Whore of Babylon, the enemy of Jehovah—in whatever throaty form, whispered into the final seconds of our last Year of the Lord. I wanted to shout it into the mouth of a stranger. I was prepared for everything by being prepared for nothing.

The crowd thickened the closer we all got to Times Square, drawn to it like human moths in all our papery costumes and with our sylvan expectations. The crush extended twenty blocks, corralled into metal barricades on both sides of every street. Police horses bucked and snorted away confetti, their eyes lit up with terror. Turgenev once wrote of a horse with "his whole body the shape of a comma," and I've never been so envious of a physical description, not because I wish I'd written it but because that's how I want my body perceived by others: literary, an act of punctuation.

Just as the countdown began, this kid in front of me looked up and dropped his head on my shoulder, taking me for a pillow. He couldn't have been older than twenty. At twenty-three, I felt ancient. I could see in his eyes that he was gone, completely unaware I was there. And just like that, it was 2000. We stared up at the fireworks going off over the billboards, the sky a wash of paint, scream joining scream to form a train of sound I'm sure vibrated loudly enough to reach Second Avenue. I didn't dare move, because the key to enjoying this moment with a stranger was for the kid to forget I was his pillow. I drifted away from him ever so slowly. I hope he found another shoulder from which to gaze at all the upward-extending mayhem, this resistance to countdowns and other endings. In a way, he and I were the same.

The lights didn't turn off in Times Square, nor did they do so five minutes later, or ten minutes later. I remember walking back downtown in a thinning crowd and everyone smiling at each other goofily, awkwardly, as if to say, *Oh well, we're all still here.* But maybe that was normal—the comedown after the high.

———

Over time, David made himself less and less available to me. Or he would look at me flabbergasted when I came by the studio. What did I want? I'm not sure I had anything left to offer him. Once when I was hard up for cash I asked him for a hundred bucks. He wasn't comfortable saying no, but he also wasn't thrilled with the idea of just giving me money, because that would make our friendship overtly transactional. I would have no problem being his muse for hire. Weren't we all sluts in some way or another, consorts in service to the American capitalist project?

At the time, David saw things differently. He wouldn't simply give me the hundred dollars, so he did what Andy Warhol had done when David had wandered into the offices of *Interview* magazine like a stray—he gave me a job. David told me about a script he was working on and asked if I wanted to write a scene. I jumped at the chance to collaborate. I don't remember much about the scene I showed him a few days later, except for its set piece: a kidney-shaped swimming pool. He told me in detail what he liked and didn't like and sent me home to rewrite. I was thrilled to be on the receiving end of his notorious perfectionism. To get my hundred bucks, I had to go to the offices of his lawyer, sign a waiver, and pick up a cheque I had no idea how to cash.

———

When I tell myself I wasn't taken advantage of when doing porn, I'm not being honest. I often conveniently forget about the very first shoot. That guy on the bicycle. I've already mentioned the shower scene, but there's a deeper story. After we'd done a bunch of nudes with me posing erect in his windowsill framed against the Twin Towers—some people have an architecture fetish, what can I say—he wanted me to pretend I had a drink. He handed me a glass of apple juice in a Mason jar and said it would look like whisky. *How vanilla,* I thought. After I imbibed some of the golden liquid, he told me to drop my dick into the glass and just let it hang there. *Snap.* I was happy with the shoot until I later found the photo set online. *This can't be the right sequence.* Here, it *started* with my dick in the empty glass, then the glass somehow filled, then I *drank* it. Oh my god. I was such a dumb whore. I think I'm most upset that I wasn't able to enjoy my watersports scene while it was happening. Because the truth is that I would have done it anyway.

Other photographers asked if they could touch me when it wasn't part of the original deal. And sometimes they didn't ask. I usually went along with it because they could replace me with other boys so easily. The worst was when I could feel myself aging out of the photographer's interest mid-shoot, becoming obsolete right in front of the camera.

———

Sometimes, to make a bit of extra cash, I sold merch on the street. Nothing sells like umbrellas in the rain. One day, I bought a few stacks of knock-off Yankees caps for two bucks each, stood in Times Square at the corner of 40th Street and

Seventh Avenue, and looked for customers. Of course, the Yankees had made the playoffs again, so I marked up the caps to eight bucks. This was capitalism at its peak, and I was at the centre of its slimy beating heart. I could see the Nasdaq ticker click up with every tourist I made happy. The only person who wasn't happy was the guy who ran the sporting goods store on the same corner I worked. He gave me the stink eye all day.

After a while I could see suckers peripherally, and I'd start my pitch without looking. Except that one time I did that to three undercover cops. They showed me their badges and asked if I had a licence, which I didn't. Then they asked me for ID, but I wasn't carrying any. They slapped on the cuffs and told me I was under arrest. I was surprised, because I'd always assumed that sex work is what would get me locked up. Yes, I would eventually leave New York, but I didn't want that to happen by deportation. They shoved me into a van that was waiting on the corner. They inspected my hats and speculated about their quality. "Damn, these are counterfeit on top of that. Hate to hear what the judge will think of this." Playfulness made their intimidation more menacing. They pretended I wasn't there while they enumerated every establishment within a mile radius of my rooming house, just to make sure I knew they had eyes on me. "That's a busy corner. There's a church right next to the bodega. We know it really well." I was terrified. And I wished I'd never tried to sell those stupid caps in the first place. How much could I have made that day, fifty bucks? Ridiculous. If I'd had my ID on me they probably would've fined me and let me go. I asked them to drive me home so that I could get my passport. "This isn't a taxi. Just sit tight."

The arresting officer—a rookie—was overzealous with my intake. He pressed my fingerprints so hard on the scanner that they smudged again and again. His supervisor laughed and told him to go easy. I spent the night in a cell with another guy, and we didn't talk much. We just sipped the cold dishwater coffee they served in the wee hours and ate our stale English muffins. "I'm a Canadian," I told the guards, as if that would save me. "It doesn't matter," they said. "You'll see the judge tomorrow." At court, I was assigned a public defender who said that if I pleaded guilty the judge would drop the misdemeanour for lesser charges, so that's the option I took. White privilege meant I got off easy. I was sentenced to a day of community service, which was genius on their part, because within a few hours I was in an orange jumpsuit, sweeping up trash on the same corner they'd caught me on. I was literally cleaning up Times Square—cleaning it of myself. Working for the mayor.

The cops claimed my baseball caps were "evidence" and kept them. But I know in my heart that they wore them when the Yankees won the championship that fall.

———

I felt the end before it came, but the end of what? My time in New York? Print porn, and how it merged two forms of tactility? I could hear the end with every digital camera click. I had an unshakable feeling that, despite the shitty new technology, once these pixels became a little less visible the end would come rushing into focus and we could either join it or be left behind. Decades later, when I was interviewed for a profile of the magazines I'd posed for, the journalist told me I was one of the few living models he could find. Queer history disappears disproportionately quickly, usually before it's documented.

I know I felt the end because I started to sell photos of myself. It wasn't so much that I needed the money. My idea of leaving New York was leaving almost everything I'd done in the city behind. It was a kind of burial. A *dust to dust*, so perhaps more of a cremation. I made a few thousand dollars through several acts of legerdemain like that, and I felt no shame. Yet I learned the hard way that trying to sell nude photos of yourself to the gallery that represents the photographer—the one who gave you the prints as a gift—is a faux pas. The gallerist told the photographer, who was furious. I sold other prints of myself to a photographer who was also a collector, and didn't make the same mistake.

I paid off some debts as part of saying goodbye. A few weeks before going back to Montreal, there was still one debt to settle. Once when I was short on rent, after I'd been paid my fee for a porn film I hit up one of the producers, Frank, for three hundred dollars. Sensing a boy in trouble, and perhaps my earnestness—a JW can never really shed themselves of that quality—he obliged. Now I wanted to pay Frank back, so I called him up and asked him out to lunch. "You choose the place, any place you like," I said, feeling grandiose. We met at a ritzy bistro in Chelsea and sat on the fenced-in terrace. "I never thought I'd see you again," he said. I wanted to show him that unlike all the other boys, I was no flake. Frank ordered a Cobb salad. "Get something else," I commanded with my new daddy voice, slapping a wad of cash on the patio table. I'd saved my greatest performance for last.

———

I don't have any selfies from this pre-selfie time in New York, and I wish I did. It's almost as if Stanley Stellar knew that would happen; he'd invited my art direction for our many shoots together, and he regularly gifted me prints. There's one I'm particularly glad I didn't sell, from that time he let me pose with a notebook and a pen. It's a black-and-white silver gelatin, eight and a half by eleven, embossed with his signature.

I'm splayed on the wood floor of Stanley's studio, shirt-less, shoeless, wearing black dress pants. My pager has fallen where I dropped it. My scuffed sneakers are scattered to the side. My black zip-up briefcase sits in the corner. I present as a cross between hobo and businessperson, which is as good a definition of hustler as I can think of. You can't see my face because it's covered by the spiral note-book. I'm doodling on its cover with my right hand. The statement is that the text in the notebook should stand in for the boy in the photo; that the half-nude body is just a meat sack in service to the writing. I'm trying to tell the viewer that my gaze is turned on *them*. Maybe I'm trying to tell Stanley—as well as myself—that I'd already left New York. It's an act of erasure more than one of declaration, but it's also one of self-avoidance. In the photo, you can smell the danger of trying to tell the story too soon, before it's even partially lived. The boy in the photo would put the notebook away and, in turning squarely to the lens, the tunnel, the avenue, fully inhabit the feeling of being lost and all it could mean before trying to describe it.

ACKNOWLEDGMENTS

Even though this book doesn't cover a complete life, it's still impossible to thank everyone who changed me in some way during the time it took to write it and to prepare to write it, or who had some other impact. There are people who don't get enough space in these pages and who deserve more, and some I'll find other ways to acknowledge. I'm lucky to know the kindest people in the world, including some whose names I've changed throughout the book. Here are a few of them.

Endless thanks:

To my agent, Akin Akinwumi of Willenfield Literary Agency, for seeing the potential in my earliest essays and for creating the conditions they needed to sprout. Your belief and passion helped me dream bigger than was ever possible. I learn so much from your scholarship.

To my editor, David Ross, for shaping the book into what it is today, for coaxing me to dig deeper, and for plucking the title out of the text, but really, out of the air. You've grown me as a writer and I'm grateful for it. To Karen Alliston for the brilliant copy edit and improvements on so many levels. To Eleanor Gasparik for proofreading. To Shona Cook for her expertise on how to put my story out into the world. To Matthew Flute for an interior and exterior design that's the perfect home for the text. And to everyone else at Penguin Random House Canada who has made this process such a joy: Nicole Winstanley, Dan French, Bonnie Maitland, and Linda Friedner.

Earlier versions of several of these essays first appeared in the following journals and magazines, some under different titles: "The Letter" in *The Rumpus*, "The Glow of Electrum" in *The Malahat Review*, "The Witness Is Complicit" in *TriQuarterly* and republished in *Literary Hub*, "Moonwalking to Armageddon" in *Maisonneuve* and republished in *Reader's Digest Canada*, and "A Library for Apostates" in *Catapult*. Parts of other essays appeared in *Electric Literature*, *The Florida Review*, and *Fourth Genre*. To Gabrielle Bellot, Joshua Bohnsack, Emma Cleary,

C. R. Foster, Madi Haslam, Iain Higgins, Laura Julier, L'Amour Lisik, Angelina Mazza, Lauren McKeon, Aram Mrjoian, Sarah Ratchford, Marisa Siegel, Jake Wolff, and Jess Zimmerman: this book would not be the same without your energy and editorial wisdom.

To Dusty Owl Press for giving me the opportunity to first write about Jehovah's Witnesses. To the team at Arsenal Pulp Press for being such an important part of my writing life for so many books. Thank you to Matthew Hays for prodding me every few years to get this memoir done.

To writers who have articulated the Jehovah's Witness experience in ways that have rejuvenated my studies and my thinking: Joy Castro, Joy Notoma, Paul Mendez, Ali Millar, and Amber Scorah. To other writers for their many gifts: Amber Dawn, Sami Basbous, Richard Burnett, Alexander Chee, Garrard Conley, Ivan Coyote, Lilly Dancyger, Samuel R. Delany, Christopher DiRaddo, Amanda Earl, Anna Gazmarian, Sarah Gerard, Garth Greenwell, Scott Heim, Jordan Kisner, Bruce LaBruce, Nate Lippens, Paul Lisicky, Greg Marshall, Derek McCormack, Amanda Montell, Patrick Nathan, Meghan O'Gieblyn, Heather O'Neill, Anakana Schofield, Sarah Schulman, Mattilda Bernstein Sycamore, Jordan Tannahill, Miriam Toews, Thomas Waugh, Tara Westover, and Zoe Whittall.

To Francisco Ibáñez-Carrasco, Marcus McCann, and David Rimmer for your brilliance and care, and for reminding me to trust my voice. To Lori Schubert and all my friends at the Quebec Writers' Federation for your ongoing good work. To Ken Harvey and Bruce Myers for your support and kindness. To Boyka Velinova and Stoyan Velinov for adventures in La Gomera and our many conversations at the writing table. To Aaron and Becky: I couldn't have lasted in Poland without your friendship.

To Stanley Stellar for helping me see myself in new ways every time. It means so much to have your photo on the cover. You are a gem. To Richard Kern, David LaChapelle, Misa, Reed Massengill, and other photographers who let me into your stunning worlds, and for reinventing our shared one many times over.

To Ricky Dennill for a lifetime of pointing me in the right direction, for being there in ways unmatched, and for encouraging me not to forget about personal growth when I was too focused on other things. I couldn't have done any of this without you. To Jair Matrim for always expanding my universe, and for your beautiful brain. To Farah Khan and Alison Slattery for inspiring me to jump deeper into the writing life without a safety net. To seeley quest for radical support in every way, and for the attentiveness of your love.

To Hyram Laurel for the drives to the beach, sheltering me on East 10th, and the nurturing that got me through the difficult times of figuring out a city as well as myself. To John Peirson for our afternoons on the balcony and the portals they've opened.

To Danny, Jude, Myles, Natalya, Paul, and Vahé for having lived an uncommon life together. We will remember Stephen and Ian in ways that would make them proud.

To Cam Martin and Sylvie Zebroff for helping round out my education, and the many small moments of care that keep me afloat. To Aileen, Erin, Diego, Dolores, Johnny, Kathy, Louise, Simon, and the aunts, uncles, and cousins in my family for your generous love. To Catrina, who has witnessed it all. What an honour to grow and change with you. I wish everyone could have a sibling so cool. I'm yours forever. I thank my mother for her love and for her survivorship.

To Mark, my love, for everything. There hasn't been a moment, whether in the desert or at a concert, when we haven't found beauty together, which I've needed. Thank you for dealing with the complicated author of this memoir and somehow resurrecting him to healing every time, and for believing.

To Wes, my love, for everything. This work grew in your care, and so did my decision to go back to school, which I can never thank you properly for. You help me feel that everything is possible, which was so important when writing a book about endings. Here's to many more beginnings together.

To fellow apostates, and all who find themselves in various states of leaving. Thank you to the many ex-JW activists whose brilliant and life-changing work makes departure a safer process.

I could not have written this book without financial support from the Conseil des arts et des lettres du Québec.

WORKS CITED/CONSULTED

BOOKS

Kyria Abrahams, *I'm Perfect, and You're Doomed*, Simon & Schuster, 2010

André Aciman, *Homo Irrealis*, Farrar, Straus & Giroux, 2021

Sarah Berman, *Don't Call It a Cult: The Shocking Story of Keith Raniere and the Women of NXIVM*, Viking, 2021

Mattilda Bernstein Sycamore, *The Freezer Door*, Semiotexte, 2020

Gary Botting and Heather Botting, *The Orwellian World of Jehovah's Witnesses*, University of Toronto Press, 1984

Joy Castro, *The Truth Book*, University of Nebraska Press, 2011

Samuel R. Delany, *Times Square Red, Times Square Blue*, New York University Press, 1999

Mark Dery, *The Pyrotechnic Insanitarium: American Culture on the Brink*, Grove Press, 1999

Sarah Gerard, *Sunshine State*, Harper Perennial, 2017

Adrian Grant, *Michael Jackson 1958–2009. Eine Bilddokumentation. Die Tribut-Ausgabe*, Bosworth Music, 2010

Bohumil Hrabal, *Too Loud a Solitude*, HarperVia, 1992

La Toya Jackson with Patricia Romanowski, *La Toya: Growing Up in the Jackson Family*, Dutton, 1991

Jordan Kisner, *Thin Places: Essays from In Between*, Macmillan, 2020

Paul Lisicky, *Later: My Life at the End of the World*, Graywolf Press, 2020

Ali Millar, *The Last Days*, Ebury Press, 2022

Amanda Montell, *Cultish: The Language of Fanaticism*, HarperCollins, 2021

José Esteban Muñoz, *Cruising Utopia: The Then and There of Queer Futurity*, New York University Press, 2009

Prince Rogers Nelson and Dan Piepenbring, *The Beautiful Ones*, Penguin Random House, 2019

Meghan O'Gieblyn, *Interior States*, Anchor, 2018

James Penton, *Jehovah's Witnesses in Canada: Champions of Freedom of Speech and Worship*, Macmillan of Canada, 1976

Jordan Schildcrout, *Murder Most Queer: The Homicidal Homosexual in the American Theater*, University of Michigan Press, 2014

Sarah Schulman, *Conflict Is Not Abuse: Overstating Harm, Community Responsibility, and the Duty of Repair*, Arsenal Pulp Press, 2016

Sarah Schulman, *Ties That Bind: Familial Homophobia and Its Consequences*, The New Press, 2012

Amber Scorah, *Leaving the Witness: Exiting a Religion and Finding a Life*, Viking, 2019

J. Randy Taraborrelli, *Michael Jackson: The Magic, The Madness, The Whole Story*, Grand Central Publishing, 2010

Tara Westover, *Educated*, HarperCollins, 2018

Numerous books and articles published by the Watch Tower Bible and Tract Society of Pennsylvania and available on JW.org were consulted.

ESSAYS, ARTICLES, INTERVIEWS

Mario Alejandro Ariza, "Come Heat and High Water," *The Believer*, November 30, 2018

"A Brief History of Killer Smurfs," *Paranormal World Wiki*, https://paranormal-world.fandom.com/wiki/A_Brief_History_of_Killer_Smurfs

Tabitha de Bruin, "Oka Crisis," *The Canadian Encyclopedia*, July 11, 2013

Lilly Dancyger, "The Queen's Gambit and the Dangerous Myth of Drug-Induced Genius," *Harper's Bazaar*, November 16, 2020

John Dart, "Jackson Out of Jehovah's Witness Sect," *Los Angeles Times*, June 7, 1987

"David LaChapelle: American Jesus," *Nowness*, July 17, 2010

Erik Davis, "What Exactly Lurks Within the Backward Grooves of 'Stairway to Heaven'?" *Salon*, June 24, 2017

Randy Dotinga, "A Mansion for the Resurrected, in Kensington," *Voices of San Diego*, June 1, 2011

Neil Drumming interviewing Will McMillan, "Kids in the Hall," *This American Life*, September 1, 2017

Camille T. Dungy, "Is All Writing Environmental Writing?," *The Georgia Review*, Fall 2018

"50 Best Michael Jackson Songs," *Rolling Stone*, June 23, 2014

C. R. Foster, "Addicted to Self-Care? Activism Is Better for Your Recovery," *HuffPost*, October 10, 2017

"The Funeral of Fr. Monsignor Alfred Mąka—for Many Years the Parish Priest of the Co-Cathedral in Ostrów Wielkopolski," *eKAI*, March 18, 2021

Peter Galvin, "Shoot to Thrill," *The Advocate*, December 8, 1998

Anna Gazmarian, "The (Loud) Soundtrack to My Struggle with Faith," *Longreads*, October 2019

Ari L. Goldman, "Dissent Grows Among Jehovah's Witnesses," *The New York Times*, August 29, 1984

Garth Greenwell, "'I Wanted Something 100% Pornographic and 100% High Art': The Joy of Writing About Sex," *The Guardian*, May 8, 2020

Nancy Griffin, "The Thriller Diaries," *Vanity Fair*, June 24, 2010

Zoë Heller, "What Makes a Cult a Cult?," *The New Yorker*, July 5, 2021

Claire Hoffman, "Prince's Life as a Jehovah's Witness: His Complicated and Ever-Evolving Faith," *Billboard*, April 28, 2016

Claire Hoffman, "Soup with Prince," *The New Yorker*, November 24, 2008

Carrie S. Ingersoll-Wood, "The Educational Identity Formation of Jehovah's Witnesses," *Religion & Education*, Taylor & Francis Online, August 12, 2022

Leslie Jamison, "Does Recovery Kill Great Writing?," *The New York Times*, March 13, 2018

Matt Jones, "The Unthinkable Fossil of Hope," *New England Review*, 40.1, 2019

Kyung Lah, "Inside Prince's Private Faith," *CNN Entertainment*, April 25, 2016

Paul Lieberman and Diane Haithman, "N.Y. Art Show Gets Scathing Giuliani Review: 'Sick Stuff,'" *Los Angeles Times*, September 24, 1999

Michael Lipka, "A Closer Look at Jehovah's Witnesses Living in the U.S.," *Pew Research Center*, April 26, 2016

Jo Livingstone, "With Michael Jackson, It's Different," *The New Republic*, March 11, 2019

John Nova Lomax, "The Year the Smurfs Attacked," *Houston Press*, July 14, 2008

Janet Maslin, "*Deathtrap* with Michael Caine," *The New York Times*, March 19, 1982

Cristina Maza, "Secret Documents Reveal Sex Abuse Scandal in Jehovah's Witnesses Church," *Newsweek*, January 10, 2018

Scott Meslow, "Will Moviegoers Ever Be Comfortable Watching Two Dudes Kiss?," *GQ*, March 17, 2017

Wesley Morris, "Michael Jackson Cast a Spell. 'Leaving Neverland' Breaks It," *The New York Times*, February 28, 2019

Michael Musto, "How Mayor Giuliani Decimated New York City Nightlife," *Vice*, March 6, 2017

"1953–59 The Supreme Court of Canada," *Canada's Human Rights History*, https://historyofrights.ca/encyclopaedia/main-events/1953-59-supreme-court-canada-civil-liberties

Douglas Quenqua, "A Secret Database of Child Abuse," *The Atlantic*, March 22, 2019

"Racial Segregation & Jehovah's Witnesses," *Avoidjw*, https://avoidjw.org/en/news/racial-segregation

"Rare Copy of Prince's Disavowed Black Album Found in Canada," *CBC News*, June 5, 2018

"Religious Landscape Study: Jehovah's Witnesses," *Pew Research Center*, 2014

Aja Romano, "Michael Jackson's 'Thriller' Is the Eternal Halloween Bop—and So Much More," *Vox*, October 31, 2018

Aja Romano, "Why Satanic Panic Never Really Ended," *Vox*, March 31, 2021

Nadja Sayej, "Gay Porn Provocateur Bruce LaBruce Gets a MoMA Show," *Maclean's*, April 16, 2015

Amber Scorah, "I Was Raised a Jehovah's Witness. When I Left the Faith, My Family and Community Shunned Me," *The Globe and Mail*, June 9, 2019

Caroline St-Pierre, "Quebec Class Action Alleging Sexual Abuse in Jehovah's Witnesses Can Proceed," *CBC News*, March 5, 2019

Valerie Stivers, "Eat This Book: A Food-Centric Interview with Amber Scorah," *The Paris Review*, July 5, 2019

Eve Thomas, "Wake-Up Call: How These Women Have Escaped Cults," *Elle Canada*, June 9, 2022

Jose Torres-Pruñonosa, Miquel-Angel Plaza-Navas, Silas S. Brown, "Jehovah's Witnesses' Adoption of Digitally-Mediated Services During Covid-19 Pandemic," *Cogent Social Sciences*, Taylor & Francis Online, February 25, 2022

Matthew Trzcinski, "Prince: The Secret Backwards Message He Hid in 'Darling Nikki,'" *Showbiz CheatSheet*, May 8, 2020

Eliot Van Buskirk, "Sorry, Perez—The New Yorker Stands by Its Prince Story," *Wired*, November 18, 2008

Luke Vander Ploeg, "Lack of Education Leads to Lost Dreams and Low Income for Many Jehovah's Witnesses," *NPR*, February 19, 2017

"Victims 'Told Not to Report' Jehovah's Witness Child Abuse," *BBC.com*, November 20, 2017

"VIP Ex-Testimoni di Geova," *Testimoni di Geova Online Forum*, https://testimonidigeova.freeforumzone.com/d/10845935/ Testimoni-di-Geova-VIP-famosi-celebri-/discussione. aspx?idm1=126188911&pl=100

"Virginia Psychologist Treats Stutterers by Computer-Assisted Therapy, but Some Experts Voice Doubt," *The New York Times*, March 27, 1972

Lawrence Weschler, "Solidarność," *Artforum*, February 1982

Jill Wherrett, "Aboriginal Peoples and the 1995 Quebec Referendum: A Survey of the Issues," *Government of Canada Publications*, February 1996

FILM, VIDEO, PODCASTS

Call Bethel, podcast series by Katherine Rushton of *The Telegraph* on *Apple Podcasts*, first uploaded June 18, 2022

Crusaders: Ex Jehovah's Witnesses Speak Out, directed by Aaron Kaufman, *Vice TV*, 2021

"Darling Nikki: Forwards . . . Then Backwards," uploaded by Steve Sorensen, April 21, 2011, www.youtube.com/ watch?v=Gnm-u4Xq9ag

"Fred Franz Speech on 1975," uploaded by TheRazorSwift, September 18, 2011, www.youtube.com/watch?v=yBwKX-5qXT0

"Prince—Super Bowl XLI—Halftime Show 2007 FULL SHOW HD," uploaded by Music Entertainment, April 14, 2017, www.youtube.com/watch?v=-WYYlRArn3g

"The Y2K Bug," episode of the *You're Wrong About* podcast by Michael Hobbes and Sarah Marshall, on *Apple Podcasts*, May 4, 2020

"Victory Tour (Montreal)—News Report—The Jacksons," uploaded by Generation Jackson, April 10, 2012, www.youtube.com/watch?v=sn7SqNKQxmE

FURTHER RESOURCES

avoidjw.org

reddit.com/r/exjw

gayxjw.org

jw.support.com

jwfacts.com

jwfaq.com